We Will Be Like Him

Growing Toward God at Every Age of Life

Vincent Rush

Paulist Press
New York / Mahwah, NJ

Cover & book design by Lynn Else

Library of Congress Cataloging-in-Publication Data

Rush, Vincent E.
    We will be like Him : growing toward God at every age of life /Vincent Rush.
        p. cm.
    Includes bibliographical references (p.   ).
    ISBN 978-0-8091-4511-9 (alk. paper)
    1. Spiritual formation. 2. Developmental psychology—Religious aspects—Christianity. 3. Maturation (Psychology)—Religious aspects—Christianity. 4. Christianity—Psychology. I. Title.
    BV4511.R83 2008
    248.4—dc22

                                                                2007032620

Published by Paulist Press
997 Macarthur Boulevard
Mahwah, New Jersey 07430

www.paulistpress.com

Printed and bound in the
United States of America

Contents

Acknowledgments   vii

Introduction   1

Chapter One: A Journey into Self-Knowledge   7

Chapter Two: How Understanding Develops   23

Chapter Three: Moral Reasoning: The Early Stages   31

Chapter Four: Postconventional Moral Reasoning   43

Chapter Five: Growing in Faith   51

Chapter Six: Psychosexual Development   64

Chapter Seven: Ego Development   78

Chapter Eight: Taking Stock   88

Chapter Nine: Spiritual Practice   97

Chapter Ten: Developmental Thinking:
         A Practical Application   108

Chapter Eleven: Putting What We Know to Work   117

Notes   124

For Further Reading   129

Beloved, we are God's children now;
what we will be has not yet been revealed.
What we do know is this: when he is revealed,
we will be like him,
for we will see him as he is.

First Letter of St. John 3:2

∾

Acknowledgments

I was looking for a simple introductory book on recent thinking about how adults change throughout life. When I expressed frustration at my lack of success to a colleague, she suggested that I write the book I was looking for. I had been teaching for some fifteen years in our diocesan Pastoral Formation Institute and had regularly heard participants' dissatisfaction with the assigned readings on this topic. I also had the hope that, if more people understood and appreciated developmental differences rather than being threatened by their manifestations, a measure of unnecessary conflict might be lifted from families and communities. Thus this book.

I would like to thank the participants in the Institute for their questions, their energy, and their courage in listening to ideas that often challenged their accustomed ways of thinking. I am grateful to the Institute's leadership for many years of delightful collaboration, and in particular to Diane Vella for starting me on this writing project and for reading the first draft; and to Edward Bacon, OSF, and Patricia Megale, the visionaries behind the Institute at its beginning. The staff of the parish of St. Hugh of Lincoln were flexible and gracious when I needed weekends with light pastoral duties so that I could lead workshops for ministers in training, and without their help the ideas here would not have taken form.

Thanks are also due to the Diocese of Rockville Centre for a sabbatical that gave me time to write; to the Louisville Institute's program of Sabbatical Grants for Pastoral Leaders for generous support; and to Dr. and Mrs. Jimmy Lim for their gift of a quiet and beautiful place to live during the time that this book took shape.

I also owe a great debt to mentors earlier along the way, most particularly to Msgr. James Coffey, who taught me a great many things about how people mature and is the source of the pub riddle in chapter one. Dr. Mary Henle was a major force in teaching me to read the psychological research literature with an eye for what mattered; I hope I have not abused her confidence here. Rev. Joseph Lynch, SM, has kept me focused on the questions that matter. Dan Connors not so many years ago encouraged me to write for publication. Maureen Jessnick, RSM, with whom I worked closely for almost two decades in the Institute, helped me by countless informal conversations to refine many of the ideas here. And friends encouraged and critiqued, and reminded me that life was larger than the attempt to capture a small slice of it in print. I thank most especially Pamela Fallon, Lauren Hanley, CSJ, Msgr. William Hanson, and Susan Moran. My gratitude to them goes beyond words.

Introduction

This is a book for people who want to appreciate how they have changed through the years and what might be still to come. The context is set by a text from the First Letter of Saint John: "We are God's children now; what we will be has not yet been revealed" (3:2). John clearly understands that, however accomplished our present state, we are not yet in our finished form. We must expect to be changed; how else could we get from what we are now to "what we will be"?

God's grace is no doubt fundamental in these changes, but grace remains mysterious and we will not dwell much on it here. Instead the discoveries of contemporary psychology, most especially a part of personality research called adult development, will mark out this book's path. But the work is not theoretical; you should be able to observe in yourself and in those around you much of what I describe here. Take a simple example:

A parent hears a crash of glass. Her young daughter—call her Amanda—toddles in, shouting, "Mommy, Eddie hitted the ball and he breaked the window!" If you are a parent you have no doubt heard your child say such things. When it happened you calmed Amanda, you went to see what had happened, you talked to Eddie, and you fixed the window. What you probably did not do was to consider: Why did she say *hitted* and *breaked*? You know well that children are different from adults. But just how are they different? Over a few years' time your child has gone from not speaking at all, to describing everything in the present tense ("Tomorrow we go mall!"), to now correctly noting that the ball was hit and the window broken in the past. And although (perhaps while repairing the window) you may despair that maturity and responsibility will ever arrive for the next generation, you also know that eventually balls will have been *hit*, not *hitted*, and windows *broken* rather than *breaked*.

A New Way of Understanding Changes

But how do such changes happen? Growing to proficiency in English is only one of a multitude of shifts that we all experience, live through, and see in others, yet rarely stop to wonder about. Are there markers that we can understand and appreciate, guideposts that we can use to find our bearings along the path of development from infancy to maturity? Is there such a thing as a final stage to maturing? Does everyone get there? You have no doubt met grownups who, having half-mastered English grammar sufficiently to know that saying "Him and me went out" is a mistake, now avoid *him* and *me* seemingly at random and proudly construct phrases such as "between he and I." An adult body and gray hair may not indicate that one is beyond the need to grow.

Careful researchers have allowed us to understand how people who say such things as these examples think. English is a mix of rules and of exceptions to those rules. Children learn the general rule for the past tense ("Add *-ed* to the verb") and overgeneralize it, not immediately recognizing that verbs such as *hit* and *break* are exceptions to the general rule and thus have to be treated differently. Adults who say "between he and I" are similarly applying what they have wrongly assumed to be some rule about the use of *him* and *me*. While it may be conventional to call such choices of words errors, this book does not take that approach. It is certainly true that *hitted* and "between he and I" do not follow the rules of standard English, but the important thing for our purpose here is that the people saying such things are doing what seems right within the world of language as they understand it. They are acting in a way that is to them natural and self-evidently appropriate. They are following the rules as they have come to understand them, only they live, we might say, in a slightly different universe of language from the rest of us. The study of adult development requires that we become detectives and investigate what appear to us to be errors or oddities, suspecting that they are clues to the sort of mental world that someone else lives in. Such a study also invites us to consider the times when life has surprised or confounded us. We can learn to consider our mistakes as evidence that we do not yet understand accurately the real social and material world we ourselves live in.

The Focus of This Book: World Building

This book does not focus on language use, but these examples from language offer clear examples of our larger theme. The keystone for understanding is that each of us is actively engaged in interacting with a world as we believe it to be, having constructed our view of the world along our journey from our first moment of awareness until today. We are in the business of making sense, of making meaning, of constructing an understanding of what the world is like. But the world one constructs is different for different people not just because of differences in experience, or culture, or social class, or gender. Nor are these differences in the worlds we construct explained when we include the varieties of temperament or of Jung's "psychological types."[1] The study of human development is a tour of some predictable ways that all human beings seem disposed first to construct their world, and then to revise and improve it, along an understandable path. It does not explain everything, of course; but it illuminates a great deal that would otherwise leave us puzzled.

This field of knowledge illuminates especially one rarely noted source of the conflicts that so often disrupt our world and our lives. We instinctively believe that others see issues and facts the way we do, and so should have similar feelings and make similar choices. So when they draw conclusions different from the ones that seem evidently right to us, we suspect those with whom we disagree of ignorance or of bad will; or at the least we are puzzled. It can be both liberating and useful to admit, as this book encourages us to, that we disagree with others sometimes because our perspectives are different—and different in a way we are largely unaware of. Understanding these different perspectives and their origins will not eliminate conflict, but understanding may make us less likely to suspect others' motives and may perhaps help us to appreciate their claims even when we do not agree.

The Design and Pace of This Book

Readers eager to get to the gist of this book may find its pace and outline puzzling. Understanding ourselves, as will become clear, is not primarily a matter of adding facts to our knowledge. Instead, in much the way we might come to appreciate a work of art, we will walk slowly around our topic, noting our shifting responses as we go. Self-understanding will grow as you work through this book, and especially as you reflect on your own life from the perspective you are learning here. We begin by exploring two different kinds of change, using a riddle, a historical example, and a common human experience. We then move progressively through researchers' discoveries about how we come to understand the physical characteristics of our world, how we make moral judgments, how we believe, how we appreciate our embodied and sexual selves, and how we hold together a coherent sense of self through all these changes. Your discoveries will accumulate along the way, especially if you look both to yourself and to others for examples of what you read about. Toward the end of the journey will come chapters on spirituality and its relationship to adult development, and on how this perspective can make our life and work with others more pleasant and effective. Each chapter has questions for reflection and discussion at its end, and there are suggestions for further reading at the end of the book. You are being invited to walk appreciatively around and through your personal history, and to discover some new perspectives on yourself and others. At the heart is a truth summed up centuries ago by the Chinese sage Confucius: "Wisdom is rooted in watching with affection the way people grow."[2]

The Personal Context

A word about the context from which I write: I am a Catholic priest, engaged for the past several decades both in parish work and in the formation of adults for ministry and discipleship. Along the way I have found the discoveries of developmental psychology immensely helpful in understanding both myself and the people I serve, and also curiously neglected in books on spiritual formation and personal growth. So while I will draw occasionally and gladly on the Catholic tradition of wisdom about human flourishing, my emphasis will be on the light this branch of psychology has to offer. I make no claims of originality in the material on personality development; all of it is culled from the research that has established this field and continues to deepen our understanding of our journey through life. While I expect that experts might find some of what follows overly simple, I have always found that the most help to people comes from their first introduction to this way of thinking. This book is written in the hope that it can be a useful companion to you on your own journey. But so as not to get lost in weighty concepts, we begin with the strange world of hitted balls.

ONE

∽

A Journey into Self-Knowledge

"You grow taller every week," said Amanda's dad as he marked her height on the doorframe. And it was true: she seemed to add inches each month, as well as multiplying the words she knew, the faces she recognized, and the foods she disliked. Amanda certainly was changing. But notice what sort of change it was: more of what was already there. Eventually Amanda would go on to grow still bigger, to learn many more words and facts, to meet still more people.

As important as these additive changes would be to her eventual flourishing as an adult, she would also have to undergo another sort of change. Call the additive changes *type one*. Call the other sort, described just below, *type two*. Some writers would call this second sort of change *transformation*. (Others would call it *conversion*, but one of the researchers we will encounter later reserves that term for a different use, so this book will avoid it.) You may have heard the words in a religious context, and that meaning can provide a clue to their wider sense. In type-two change (or transformation) one does not simply add new facts to a collection; the meaning of the facts themselves changes as things are seen from a new perspective. In religious transformation one may shift from seeing one's life as a meaningless accident or a burden to seeing it as a gift and an invitation from a generous God. All the details of that life remain the same, but they are now all seen in a new light and have a new meaning. But this second sort of change does not happen only in large and dramatic ways. For a simple example we can use an Irish pub riddle:

> A man without eyes
> saw plums on a tree.
> He neither took plums nor left plums;
> now, how can that be?

How can that be? There is a simple solution to the riddle, and it does not involve any metaphorical use of words or any similar sort of trick. The words are literally used, and the solution is straightforward. You do not need more information. It is just that the solution is now—unless you know the riddle already or have just figured it out—unimaginable. Your perception of how the riddle's elements fit together will have to shift for you to discover the solution.

If the answer to the riddle did not immediately come to you (and for most people it does not), take a minute to think of how your situation now differs from what it will be when you finally know the answer. When you discover the solution you will have added a new fact to your knowledge, yes; but something else more important will have happened. You will never be able to go back to your present state of *not* knowing the answer. In a tiny way the new fact will have caused a shift in you, so that you look at this small part of the world, this riddle, differently. The solution will be obvious from this new perspective. Even if you forget the answer and someday in an Irish pub someone puts this riddle to you again, you will not be in the situation you are in now. You will say, "I know the answer to that! I just cannot think of it now!" You will not be puzzled as you now are, but only frustrated that you cannot remember from what perspective the riddle's answer becomes clear. And remembering is different from making the discovery in the first place.

How Transformations Change Us

Getting the point of a joke or a riddle is a miniature example of type-two change. Unlike Amanda's getting taller or learning new words, which do not change her in any fundamental way, as she grows she will also undergo some fundamental, transformational, type-two changes. These will shift her perspective on herself and on her world in small or, less often, large ways. Adding facts does not automatically bring about this transformational change for her, or for you. You could study all you wish about eyes, plums, trees, and Irish pubs and not be guaranteed to get the point of that riddle. Something else, something slightly mysterious, has to happen. And that something else can never be forced or guaranteed. You know this; in the past you may have tried to explain a joke or a riddle to someone and, even though he or she could repeat your words back to you, you knew the person still did not "get it." That flash of understanding cannot be created by anyone for anyone else; all an outsider can do is to make it more likely that the mysterious flash of insight will happen. (I can do that for you with the riddle by giving you a hint. But let us save that for a bit later.)

An Example of Transformation in History: A Sun-Centered World

It may help in understanding type-two change or transformation to look at an example from history. One good example is the shift from an earth-centered to a sun-centered theory of the apparent movements of the stars and planets. Before the sixteenth century their changing positions could be accurately understood and predicted even though it was assumed that the earth was the central point around which everything else revolved. Although his theory was complicated, the Greek astronomer Ptolemy (ca. AD 85–ca. 165) had accounted well for what people observed in the heavens. Ptolemy's theory was not replaced because of errors in its predictions or because of the accumulation of additional facts; it was undone by a shift of people's imagination, confirmed in part by the discovery that Jupiter's moons revolved around that planet. This was a new perspective on how bodies in the heavens moved. That movement became visible for the first time only with the invention of the telescope. But the shift from an earth-centered to a sun-centered view of the solar system did not add a new fact: it rearranged all the old ones so that things were imagined from a new perspective. This is a type-two change, transformation. When an astronomer or a person in the street got the point that what seemed to happen through the course of every day was not the movement of the sun from eastern horizon through the skies to western because of the motion of the sun around the earth, but was a result of the earth's rotation; and when she understood that the earth was in fact revolving around the sun; with those insights she left behind not a set of once-believed facts but a way of seeing and understanding. The facts shifted their relationship to one another because of the new context in which they now appeared.

This is a type-two change. And notice that once we have undergone this shift, it is somewhat artificial to go back to the old way of perceiving things. You may lie on the beach in summer and "watch the sun move" overhead, but a part of you knows that you are willingly surrendering to the spectacle of what you see; you will not puzzle, as our ancestors did, about what would bring the sun back to the East during the night to prepare it for its journey through the skies once again tomorrow. Our culture has gone through a shift in understanding; you and I have absorbed this shift into ourselves by growing up with a sun-centered perspective on the solar system. And while we may choose to visit in idle fantasy the past conception of an earth-centered universe, we can only go there as tourists; residence is forever closed to us.

Here is a clue for the pub riddle: Think about plurals. Does this help? Once you have got the point, you will see that it is crucial. If you do not yet have the solution, it may not yet seem to be the pointer it is. But if you are still puzzled, you can at least rule out certain approaches to a solution, and thus you may be able to appreciate that hints which give direction to our thought can help to bring about type-two change. Now, because of the hint, you know a bit about what sort of solution to look for.

Another Transformation: Discovering Romantic Love

A personal transformation will happen to Amanda in a few years when the converging forces of hormonal changes within her, cultural influences around her, and some cute classmate will introduce her to what she until that moment might only have read about in teen magazines and understood as an outsider: romantic love. This is another example of type-two, transformational change. Before that moment Amanda might have been puzzled by her older cousin's endless phone conversations about boys; and she might have struggled to follow the plots of television dramas without comprehending a key part of the characters' motivations. Her falling in love for the first time does not add any new facts to her knowledge; but it does rearrange her attitudes toward certain classmates who now become romantic possibilities. It lets her understand drama, from soap opera to *Romeo and Juliet,* in a new way; and it marks a stage in her psychosexual maturation.

We shall come back to the topic of romantic love in a later chapter; here we want to examine falling in love simply as an example of type-two change. It may be that some facts are added to our store of knowledge, but that is not the main thing about this, or any, transformation. The key change is in my perspective on some wider or narrower dimension of my life and who I am. And after that change, whether it happens in an instant or over the course of weeks or months, I cannot go back. Amanda may well fall out of love with her classmate in a day or an hour, or they may date through college and form a lifelong bond. But in either case, Amanda's perspective on herself and on her life has shifted permanently.

The Structure of Transformational Change

It is time to take stock of what transformational change is about. In her book *The Passionate God* Rosemary Haughton describes four elements of transformation:

- The ground needs to be prepared for the shift—by the accumulation of new experiences and images (such as with the shift to a sun-centered solar system), or pressures that may come from inside or outside us or both (as with Amanda's discovery of romantic love), or simply by felt inadequacy in the face of a challenge that life throws at us (as perhaps for you in the case of the pub riddle).

- There is usually a "weak spot" that prepares the way for the change; it could be the new discoveries made possible by the telescope, Amanda's involvement with her girlfriends in discussing romantic teen novels, or simply the puzzlement you feel so distinctly at being flummoxed by a simple-seeming riddle.

- There is a central moment of breakthrough that resists full explanation: Why this person as the beloved, and why now? What happens when one gets the point of a riddle? What did Galileo see with his imagination more than with his eyes when he confirmed the heliocentric theory of Copernicus? The shift is undeniable, but this central moment cannot be captured in words.

- Once the shift has occurred, there may be a time of consolidation but there is no going back to the way things were.[1]

(This may be a good time to return to our riddle. You can find the answer at the end of this chapter. Once you discover the solution, which may occur when you read it but takes more than simple reading, you will see this four-step process in action, especially the indescribable moment of insight and the permanence of the shift. Once you know, you know, and cannot go back to your earlier perspective.)

Using "Mistakes" to Reveal Differences in Perspective

This inability to go back to an earlier way of viewing things is why it was important to notice the oddness of Amanda's language when she said Eddie *hitted* the ball. Simply to call it a childish mistake is to fail in the role of good detective. Amanda believes she is correct. Her use of the form *hitted* is a clue to what her world of language is like. If we are to understand the world the way it now seems to her, we need to appreciate that she is living and acting according to the rules of her world, the only world she can know, and it is clearly not the same world as our own. Even though we all once lived there, we cannot now go back to live in that world of overgeneralized past tenses that she now inhabits. But we can seek to understand it, even if only from the outside.

When Amanda makes a choice different from the one that seems right to us, we are presented with a clue to her world. And while it may be only a minor accomplishment for us to appreciate her not-yet-complete grasp of irregular verb tenses, it is much more substantial to take to heart what this exercise suggests: that our own present world is not that much unlike Amanda's in one very vital way. You and I also live mentally in a world that we have constructed, and act according to what we believe are the rules of that world.

Although we cannot help assuming that *our* world is *the* world, appreciating Amanda's situation might help us break loose from that naïve assumption. We do not perceive and understand the world as it truly is, but rather according to our construction of it at this moment. We might of course sympathize with Amanda as immature, as she is; we might say that of course her grasp of the world is incomplete, which it is; we might expect that as she matures her sense of the world will begin to resemble ours more fully, which it probably will. But we might do all these things and still wrongly suppose that as Amanda's view of the world converges with our own, it is at the same time inevitably converging on a view of the world as it truly is. And while we may hope that this is true, we must not evade the conclusion that our own view is still a personal and partial construction. It is adequate no doubt for many tasks, probably more accurate than Amanda's, but it is not in any way the final word.

This is not to deny that there is a real, objective, external world that we all live in; but each of us knows that world only partially and according to our own construction of it. This is something that sages have known all along. It was a maxim of Saint Thomas Aquinas (ca. 1225–1274) that whatever we perceive is shaped by our readiness to perceive it.[2] What seems from one perspective to be a "mistake" probably makes sense from another point of view. And so we will need to act like detectives and investigate occasions when we are surprised by our disagreements with others if we are ever to appreciate and understand the different worlds that people, including you and me, live in.

> *You and I also live mentally in a world that we have constructed, and act according to what we believe are the rules of that world. We cannot help assuming that* our *world is* the *world. And simply adding information will not make our world more adequate in a fundamental way.*

If we are to take the findings of adult development seriously, or even to trust Saint John when he says "what we will be has not yet been revealed" (1 John 3:2), we have to admit that even though we cannot imagine it now (just as

Amanda cannot imagine being in love before it happens to her), there is a perspective on ourselves and the world that is more complete and adequate than our present one. We will have to assume, at least for the sake of this inquiry, that simply adding information will not make our world more adequate in a fundamental way. Type-one change is not enough. We will have to entertain the possibility that we need to undergo one or many transformations if our perspective on ourselves and on the world is to become more mature and more accurate.

Embeddedness and Worldviews

The psychologist Robert Kegan offers a useful image to describe the need for transformation. He describes each of us as *embedded* in our worldview.[3] The one thing we cannot do is to understand our present perspective "from the outside," seeing it in relationship to ourselves. Just as a pebble in a concrete sidewalk is embedded within the sidewalk, similarly each of us is embedded in a way of viewing the world. Only by moving to a new and more inclusive view—from above the sidewalk, as it were—can we act with freedom in regard to situations that once stymied us. Before you understood the riddle you were unable to see the connections that you now do; those connections, obvious from your present perspective, make the solution to the riddle transparent. The rhyme is now no longer a riddle, and for you never will be again. Development is a sequence of such steps away from views within which we were previously embedded, toward more comprehensive views that give us the distance and perspective to act in new and more effective ways.

Of course few people actively think about such changes unless they are researchers in adult development. Most of us live through the changes and do not stop to notice how we have changed. This book is an invitation to stop and to appreciate those changes that have taken place along our life's journey, and to appreciate the transformations in our perspectives, so that we can learn to understand ourselves and others more gracefully and gently. It might also prepare us to expect more such transformations in our own and everyone's future, although of course we cannot understand them until we enter the new worlds they open to us. We can understand only what we can look back on; we can look back only because we have moved beyond. Before we inhabit a new world it is unknown territory, even if we hear it described by those who have been there. When we live within it we cannot gain the objectivity we need because we have no distance from it. Only when we gain such distance, emerging from our embeddedness by moving beyond our former worldview, can we see clearly who we once were and what sort of world we thought we lived within. Think of a set of concentric circles, like a dart board, and of life's journey as a set of steps away from the smallest, central circle. We can look back, to some degree, into the world we have left behind; but we cannot yet comprehend what the next, larger circle may contain.

Development is a sequence of steps away from views within which we were previously embedded, toward more comprehensive views that give us the distance and perspective to act in new and more effective ways.

Different Worldviews:
Random or Progressive?

If we accept the idea that people see the world differently because each of us has constructed a view of it from our unique history, we are left with this question: Is each view like a separate dot in a landscape, a dot placed seemingly at random and within no discernable larger order or pattern? Or is there a path that connects the dots in some meaningful way? Researchers who study development have found what seems to be stable and perhaps universal pathways that link some common perspectives and the transformations that shift them one into the next. The later chapters in this book will explore those paths; but here we need first to take a moment to think about the idea of stages in life.

It would be convenient but oversimple to think that particular sorts of perspectives could be grouped by their common features into life stages, and that then those stages would appear not unlike stepping stones across a creek, with the transformations like the little jumps that move us from one stable footing to the next. People are complicated, and changes often are not instantaneous, so we need to be cautious about such easy imagery. But it does nonetheless seem that there are both periods of relative stability of viewpoint along our journeys, and times of comparatively rapid change. So those who formed the language of human development have been drawn, sometimes reluctantly, to speak of stages and of transitions between stages. This language is useful shorthand, and will appear over and over in what follows. But it is important right at the beginning to note that while stages can be identified by stable patterns of perception, understanding, and action, they also shade one into the next.

Amanda will someday stop forming improper past tenses like *breaked*; but while in looking back we will see in her use of language a time of overgeneralized forms and then later a time of correct ones, we will never put our finger on one particular Tuesday morning on which the shift from one stage to another took place. Even if she becomes love-struck with a classmate at some quiet moment in one afternoon's earth science class, still the development from a stage of not appreciating such attraction into a stage of its being a significant thread in her life will not take place in days or even months. Stages and transformations are simplifications, necessary like a flashlight to illuminate life's journey so that we can understand it better; but they should not be made into rigid boxes to which people are assigned. Becoming comfortable with using the language of stages and transformations is sort of like riding a bicycle: One can fall off on one side, making the stages so distinct that violence is done to people by putting them into mental cubicles; or one can fall off on the other, keeping things so vague and uncertain that nothing useful can be understood. Like riding a bicycle, using this language well comes through practice.

Adult Development: A Recent Idea

But before we turn to the accomplishments of researchers, there is one more preliminary: the idea of adult development itself. The examples of language development have come from our childhoods. Is the sort of adulthood one attains at twenty or twenty-five a final stage beyond which no more transformations can be expected?

For centuries most people thought so. The idea of distinctive periods in adult life, or at least the study of such periods, is relatively new. Even the idea that children are not just little adults disappeared only surprisingly recently. Catholics of a certain still-living generation may remember being taught that the "age of reason" (at which children could be considered, for the purposes of law and responsibility, adults) was only age seven. Up until the nineteenth century British criminal law allowed for seven-year-olds to be punished as adults—such as being hanged for picking a pocket—although it appears that good sense prevailed and that no one that young was in fact executed, at least in recent times. The nineteenth and early twentieth centuries saw the beginnings of developmental thinking about stages of childhood, notably in the work of Sigmund Freud (1856–1939), with his stages based on zones of gratification: oral, anal, phallic, latency, and finally genital. This psychoanalytic conception did not go unchallenged (and is today somewhat discredited), but it provided a spur to what followed. The Swiss psychiatrist Carl Jung (1875–1961), an early colleague of Freud, spent much of his later independent career studying the changes in adults, becoming perhaps the first modern theorist of adult development. His conceptions of "midlife" and the "second half of life" have become fixtures of contemporary thinking.

Adult development featured prominently in the work of the later psychoanalyst Erik Erikson (1902–1994). Along with Daniel Levinson (1920–1994), whose major work *The Seasons of a Man's Life* was popularized in the widely read *Passages* by Gail Sheehy, Erikson's work opened up the idea that adult life was a continuing series of challenges which had to be navigated successfully in order to arrive at a level of full maturity. Both Levinson and Erikson focused largely on the interaction of the growing adult individual with the challenges presented by the person's culture; thus the theories they created are sometimes called *psychosocial* theories of development. Erikson's work especially laid a foundation for the work of several of the researchers whose work fills the following chapters. But before we go to them, we need to turn to Europe and the work of a man who did not call himself a psychologist at all. To understand the sort of thinking that underlies much of the work in this book, we have to return to appreciating the apparent errors of children, this time not with language, but on intelligence tests in the schools of early-twentieth-century France.

Questions for Reflection and Discussion

Understanding an idea is quite a bit like getting the point of a riddle. A moment of insight leads to understanding; the accumulation of facts helps, but it is not enough. Thus a partner in conversation can be both a guide and a challenge in coming to understand. The questions that follow the chapters are meant to help the conversation to begin. If you are reading this book in a group you might start with these, but please do not end with them; seek to link your own past experience and understanding to what you read here. If you are reading the book by yourself, consider the text your conversation partner. In either case you can gently observe yourself as you struggle to understand, and watch the process of type-two change at work in you.

1. Can you remember a few major turning points in your life that changed how you saw and understood yourself and the world? Make a list of three or four, if you can. Try to locate the four circumstances Haughton suggests: supportive circumstances, weak spot, breakthrough, and time of consolidation.

2. If you were to tell the story of your life so far, what would the chapter titles be? How would you divide your life into major segments? As you look back and learn, have the more important changes in your life been the outer events or the inner understandings?
3. What examples other than the story of Galileo can you think of for type-two or transformational change throughout history? Can you think of any in your own life?

Answer to the Pub Riddle

The man has one eye. So he is without eyes (plural—he has only one), yet can see the plums. There are two plums. He takes one, leaves the other. Thus he does not take or leave plums (plural), since he takes only one and leaves only one.

TWO

✑

How Understanding Develops

A few years before Eddie *hitted* the ball he might have spent an afternoon in a child study lab. There he would have had experiences that would be, if we were able to have them now, fascinating and perhaps terrifying. To Eddie as his infant self, they were normal. A favored toy would go out of existence as an obstacle was placed in front of it, and then burst back into being when the intruding item was removed and the toy was once again in his sight. Of course, Eddie would not know he was in such a lab, nor would the experience of items going out of existence and bursting back again be at all unusual to him. Thanks to the work of a curious adult in the early part of the twentieth century, we now know that this is the world of infants everywhere.

Jean Piaget (1896–1980) was a Swiss researcher who puzzled over how children arrived at their "wrong" answers on the intelligence tests it was his job to administer. He noticed that children of similar ages made similar mistakes, so he began to pay close attention to how the children's thinking had led them to their choices. His crucial insight was that the answers seemed right to the children, within the world as they understood it. Their answers were not randomly wrong, but had a pattern to them. The pattern arose

23

from the way the children had constructed their sense of what the world was like and how the world functioned.

Piaget's discovery led him to a program of research which mostly involved watching and listening to children very carefully while exposing them to everyday occurrences, and noting their explanations and reactions. This showed him that very young children are not at first aware of elementary aspects of the world around them, such as that things remain in existence even when they are out of sight. (The infant delighted by a game of "peekaboo" with her mother is like a little scientist, experimenting with still-novel aspects of a permanent world—in this case, her mother.)

Through careful experimentation Piaget discovered a regular series of steps that all infants and children take in constructing a sense of what the world is like.[1] At each step the child constructs a mental picture (called a *schema*) which has a logical but incomplete structure to explain and predict experience. Children are not aware of having a schema, of course, just as we are unaware of the background assumptions we rely on to make sense of our world. "Wrong" answers make sense within the child's schema; but the schema itself does not accurately reflect all the aspects of how the world really works. And because the world of experience sometimes surprises the child by not responding the way the child expects, these internal pictures of the world are put under pressure to change. Infants quickly learn to modify their expectations and to anticipate that things and people stay around even when out of sight. They revise their schema. And this is what we have called a type-two change, a transformation in the infant's understanding of the world.

The Infant: Embedded in Her Perceptions

Note again that the infant is not simply adding information, although that is certainly also going on. Accumulating experiences of objects disappearing and then reappearing are, in themselves, type-one change: The infant is adding facts. But the infant without a type-two transformation regarding the meaning of these facts is still embedded in his or her perceptions. Perception by itself seems to demonstrate that when a thing is visible, it exists; no visual image, no existence. The infant will have to emerge from this embeddedness to discover that continuing existence (what Piaget calls object permanence) is a more accurate way to understand how things in the world behave.

Thus if Eddie were to return to the lab in a few years and see a clear jar with some colored liquid in it, he would have no doubt that the jar would stay there if someone covered it with a cloth. Long ago he would have achieved object permanence, and known that things stay in existence even when out of sight. But he might well surprise us if we tried something else. For if we had him watch us empty that jar first into a clear tall, thin flask, and then that flask back into a clear, short, fat one, we could ask him: Did the tall, thin flask have more liquid, or the short, fat one? Eddie would be confident: The tall, thin one had more. (After all, the liquid went up higher.) We could thus discover that Eddie, like all children at this particular developmental stage, still lives in a world far different from ours. He can reason in certain ways, noting the height of the liquid as higher or lower in the two flasks; but he cannot yet share in our own world by seeing that the volume has always remained the same. Eddie now lives in a world different from the one he constructed in infancy, but he continues to live in a world strangely different from our own.

Piaget called his field of research *genetic epistemology*: the study of how our ways of knowing change as we develop. He, his colleagues, and researchers following in their line of thought have developed an elaborate picture of the steps children go through as they come to a mature way of thinking, and of the process of change that leads from stage to stage. The details of Piaget's research would take us away from our main interest. But it may be helpful to outline the process of change, and the stages as he discovered them, for his research was the spur and foundation for much that will occupy us in the rest of this book. The ages given here are typical; attaining the stage depends not on the child's age, but on her or his ability to perform the sort of reasoning appropriate to that stage.

Piaget's Stages of Reasoning

- *Sensorimotor stage* (birth–2 years old): The child is embedded in his or her reflexes. What things look or feel to be is so immediate that the child cannot step back to understand that things are more than how they are experienced. Children at this stage can be said to "think by doing," exploring the world around them.
- *Preoperational stage* (ages 2–5): The child needs concrete physical situations in order to "think." While Eddie can understand the word *milk* even if no milk is in sight, his thought will still be largely embedded in his perceptions. Thus he will be convinced that the tall, thin jar must have more liquid in it because the level is higher.
- *Concrete operations* (ages 6–10): As the child has more experience with the world, he or she starts to form concepts and to create logical rules that explain his or her physical perceptions. Eddie will know that the volume of liquid remains the same no matter what its shape; but he

will not yet be able to think in, or explain to himself in, abstract terms about why this is so. He cannot yet think about his own thinking.

- *Formal operations* (beginning at around age 11): This marks the child's attainment of cognitive structures like those of a typical adult. At this point Eddie will be comfortable with abstract, conceptual reasoning. (Note that not all adults attain formal operational thinking; some remain at the stage of concrete operations.)[2]

Children progress through the stages always in the same order, without skipping steps; and once a stage's understanding has been reached, children do not return to previous stages. They also seem to lose the ability to understand that they had ever seen the world in such a limited way as they previously did. If we had made a video recording of Eddie confidently choosing the tall, thin jar as having more, and then had shown him the video a few months later after he had achieved what Piaget called conservation of volume, he would not believe that he was the child being shown. "No one," he would say, "could make such a silly mistake." He might even accuse the researcher of altering the video. And so we adults too have to rediscover through research the limits of childhood schemas, for we cannot recall how the world appeared to us before we came to know such things as that objects remain in existence even when we cannot see them or that volumes do not change when they change their shape.

Implications of Piaget's Discoveries

Piaget's research with children sparked a new way of thinking about development: he focused not so much on the external social challenges children were facing (as did Erikson) as on the way in which they constructed knowledge internally. Eddie was following his own sort of inner logic at the time he said that the tall jar had more liquid. His logic would eventually shift because it did not make consistently good predictions about how the real world operated. (I recall hearing that children understand the true nature of volume more quickly if the experiment is done not with liquid but with M&M candies, which seem dramatically to increase children's motivation to understand "more" and "less" accurately.) But Piaget focused on the logical pattern within the child's mind at each stage, and the way in which each child was actively constructing a world for himself according to that logic. "Mistakes," as both Eddie and we would now unthinkingly call them from a more developed perspective, were for Piaget primarily windows into the logic of the child's world.

This way of appreciating the different mental worlds in which one can live would soon be extended to research on adults, although Piaget himself did not take this step. The researchers we will meet in later chapters focused on changes that can go on throughout the lifetime, as well as expanded the range of study beyond logic to other dimensions of living. This line of thinking and research is often called *psychostructural* or *constructive-developmental* thinking, since its focus is on the internal constructions by which we all make sense of what we experience.

Conflict and Developmental Understanding

Notice how this way of thinking helps us to understand something that might until now have been perplexing. Between adults and teenagers, and even between adults, conflicts sometimes arise that make it seem as if the people involved are not living in the same universe. Developmental thinking suggests that while in one sense people do (of course) share the same universe with its physical laws and relationships, in a more important sense we may not live in a shared "world." Each of us lives within our own constructed world, and each world has a logic of its own. Some aspects of our internal constructions are no doubt similar to the constructions of other people, since we have to live together in the real world; but other aspects may well differ. By the time a person reaches adulthood, conclusions such as Eddie's about the liquid are forgotten in one's past; but in matters of moral decision making, of responsibilities to other people and to society and to God, individuals can differ dramatically based on levels of development and how they perceive the world. And then the stage is set for confusion unless we become aware that what looks to be "the same" to one person appears as "more" or "less" to another. We enter the world of adult differences through the door of moral choices, where so many contentious arguments leave opposed parties suspecting that their adversaries have to be either bad-willed or obtuse, or that they live on another planet. The first two conclusions may well be wrong and unfair; the third, metaphorically more accurate than the contestants would ever suspect.

Questions for
Reflection and Discussion

1. Have you had experiences with children that you can now see as evidence that they perceive the world far differently from the way you do as an adult?

2. Can you recall a time when you asked a young child to explain something to you, and found yourself puzzled by the answer? What was different from the way an adult might go about giving an explanation?

3. Is the idea that each of us constructs a mental picture of what the world is like novel to you? What feelings accompany this book's suggestion that your own present picture of what the world is like is partial and incomplete?

THREE

❧

Moral Reasoning:
The Early Stages

Eddie and Amanda are upstairs awake in their beds at a time they would usually be asleep; and asleep they would be, except for the loud conversation coming up from downstairs. Their parents have had friends over for dinner, and the talk has turned to the rightness or wrongness of the death penalty. As with many controversies in our society, the discussion over dinner gets nowhere. One couple, George and Martha, are firm supporters, arguing that the country's lawmakers reflected the will of the people and that duly convicted criminals have a debt to society that can sometimes be paid only with their lives. Sharon and Frank are equally firm that America is an outcast society in the community of nations, the only advanced country still to have the death penalty. Both couples can and do turn to statements of their church to support their positions. Michelle and Tim, the uneasy hosts, can see the logic of both sides but are uncomfortable, not just because the conversation has turned tense, but because they have a vague sense that something is being left out of the mix. The evening ends with no one's mind having been changed; but George was struck by Michelle's question whether any society's laws are the last word, and he hurried the evening to

31

a close because that thought was making him restless in a way he did not like but could not shake off.

The issue could be abortion, preemptive war, or voting for or against the next school budget. So many of our conflicts seem to get nowhere, with contending people and groups using the same words but seeming to mean different things by them. Nothing in this chapter will resolve any of those conflicts, and in fact our concern will be not with the substantial rightness or wrongness of any position, important as that question is in its proper place. A crucial step in the research that interests us here was the making of just this distinction between the *content* of what people judge to be right and wrong, and the mental *structure* by which they think their way to their conclusions. The focus here is on the structure, the "how" of moral reasoning, not the "what" of conclusions. Our purpose is to understand the ways in which people make moral decisions, not the content of those decisions. Research in this area was begun by someone following in Piaget's footsteps, Lawrence Kohlberg (1927–1987).[1]

Stages of Moral Reasoning

By posing moral dilemmas in careful interviews to large numbers of young men (the research was later extended to women), Kohlberg and his colleagues discovered that people reasoned differently at different stages in development from childhood and even through adulthood. The basic division (which will figure prominently in following chapters) is among what he called *preconventional*, *conventional*, and *postconventional levels* of thinking, each level split into two stages. Readers interested in gender issues may want to know that Kohlberg's research was criticized by a former colleague, Carol Gilligan.[2] She argued that girls and women make moral decisions on a somewhat different basis than do boys and men. There is now considerable agreement that Gilligan's criticism had merit, but that the general outline of Kohlberg's stage theory applies to both sexes. The stages and levels are laid out, somewhat simplified, in Table 1:[3]

Table 1. Stages of Moral Reasoning

Level	Stage	Pays attention to:
Preconventional	1	External authority that can give pain or pleasure
	2	Short-term fairness of exchange with others
Conventional	3	Expectations of others close at hand; role one is expected to play
	4	Law, rules, societal obligations
Postconventional	5	Prior-to-society values
	6	Universal values, rights, and norms

Moral Reasoning: The Preconventional Stages

The earliest moral choices that Amanda and Eddie made were just like the earliest choices of Michelle and Tim and of their dinner guests, and like yours and mine as well when we were very young. They were based on hope for pleasure and fear of punishment. Rules were all-important;

intentions did not enter in. This is Kohlberg's *stage one* of moral development. As Eddie and Amanda grew they left this stage behind; childhood was time for the refrain of "It isn't *fair!*" While Michelle and Tim tired of hearing that phrase from their children, they might have been consoled had they known that it was a sign of moral development. Eddie and, later, Amanda were becoming aware of other people's interests, and had begun to see morality as the balancing of individuals' short-term wants and desires: Kohlberg's *stage two*. They would still be considered to be at a preconventional developmental level (although some grownups still live at this stage two, and a few adults—for whom prisons are designed—even at stage one), but their ability to recognize that others have legitimate needs and interests would be the foundation for their entrance into the sorts of shared responsibilities that allow a society to function. As they grew up, this awareness would become in them the basis for conventional-level decision making.

Note here, however, that the transitions from punishment-based to fairness-based and then to future levels of decision making are not smooth, although even children know clearly when one has made the shift or has not (although they of course would not be able to describe this awareness in words). Eddie's baseball teammates, trading baseball cards on the basis of stage two fair exchange, will show contempt for a teammate still at stage one who cheats because he wrongly anticipates being able to get away with it. Because his teammates have moved beyond punishment-based thinking, they can now no longer enter sympathetically into it even to understand it. They can only respond that the cheat is not acting fairly. And their contempt will, over time, be a spur to the cheater to "learn to play fair": that is, to transform his moral thinking to a more developed level.

Content and Motive, Age and Stage

Note also that the content of the decision can be separated from the motive as we try to understand decision making. Eddie's teammate might have been scrupulously honest with his cards out of fear he would be caught and punished for cheating, but he still would have been operating out of stage one reasoning. Coming to what an outsider might see as the right moral conclusion about which sort of action to take is no measure of the stage of moral thinking that led to the conclusion. And while more developed stages of decision making might, we would hope, lead to better decisions (and certainly make for a smoother-functioning society with less need for police on every corner), they do not automatically preserve a person from bad moral choices. Maturing through levels of moral development is not the same as progress from sinner to saint. At any level of moral development one is liable to self-deception, self-interest, fear, and all the vices that have been described by thinkers throughout history. Development in moral reasoning is, again, more a matter of how any virtue or vice will be understood, not whether or not it will affect one's choices.

This is a good time to address what you may have found frustrating so far: that while it may sometimes be possible to infer something about Eddie's or Amanda's or their friends' ages, those ages are rarely mentioned. This is because our desire to link maturation with years on a calendar leads us astray. While there are typical ages for many of the developmental stages of childhood, what matters for understanding is not the age but the abilities and limitations of the child who lives in that sort of world. Children of the same chronological age can be at different stages (like Eddie's teammates); and when we think about development in adulthood a focus on chronological age can only lead us astray since it is practically irrelevant.

Conventional Moral Reasoning

But adults are often at higher stages of development than children, and the couples who kept Eddie and Amanda awake that night were no longer at a preconventional level of moral thinking. The argument over the death penalty had not been conducted on the basis of "an eye for an eye," or of allowing revenge by a victim's family. (That such arguments are occasionally heard is a sign that preconventional thinking is not rare in adults.) Instead the dinner guests made constant reference to a social system of laws and responsibilities. They had passed through stage two short-term fairness and even through the first of the conventional level stages: *stage three* interpersonal thinking (in which decisions are based on what intimates expect of you, or what is expected in your role as child or parent or kin or neighbor). They are, at the point of the conversation we overheard, at Kohlberg's *stage four*.

They are not only reasoning in a way that makes them suitable neighbors; they are the sort of people who create, by their decisions and their commitments, neighborhoods and civic associations and the larger society. Their moral universe builds, and is built around, institutional commitments, from their marriages to their occupations to their political involvements. In this they are slightly different from what we might expect. Stage three thinking (based, remember, on responsibilities of kinship role or the expectations of those closest to us) is also common in adults, although we did not hear it at this party. With an ear tuned to the difference between stage three interpersonal and stage four institutional embeddedness, one can hear the different worldviews speaking simply by listening carefully to the sorts of arguments advanced for any number of controversial issues of the day—if, that is, one has developed to stage four thinking oneself.

We should also be cautious about listening simply for the words people use. People who say, "It isn't fair!" may well be reasoning at a level beyond stage two. The phrase may be simple habit, or may refer in the speaker's mind to a larger sense of fairness than the short-term exchange of stage two. It may, for instance, imply the violation of a role expectation (stage three), or of a law (stage four). The reasoning, not the wording, reveals the speaker's perspective.

We can take a moment to understand these two stages of conventional-level moral thinking better. Stage three is based on a shift away from the short-term and individualistic interpersonal fairness of stage two into a recognition that people are often related in stable ways. That is, we have roles to play in one another's lives. The commitments and feelings and expectations of others play a part in stage three moral reasoning because the stage three person needs to consider himself to be a good friend, or brother or sister, or classmate, or neighbor—and to be thought of that way by other people important to him or her. But the focus is still embedded in the interpersonal realm; it has not yet developed any ability to step outside that world to consider the abstract, impersonal structures or systems that are embodied in the institutions of society. This ability to reason on the basis of abstractions will be a marker of stage four.

The Enlarged Moral Universe

Notice the way in which the moral universe which we consult has enlarged as we develop: stage one reasoning was entirely egocentric: pleasure versus pain for me. Stage two recognized individual other people as having interests different from my own which had to be negotiated; hence the emphasis on fairness. Stage three enlarged my vision so that

I took into account how others saw me: I had responsibilities as a child or a parent or a member of some intimate group, and those duties had to play a role in my decisions. At stage four the individuality of the others, and even my own, has been submerged by concern to fulfill the roles and responsibilities society—an abstract organization of many individuals including myself and my loved ones—imposes.

Of course, at stage four there may be conflict over which society is relevant to any decision. In our example George and Martha argue for the death penalty from a vision of a society that stops at our shores; Sharon and Frank, against it from a larger society that includes other nations as well. Which perspective is correct or even relevant does not concern us here; but we can see, even if the contestants do not, that they are at least arguing within a shared mental universe. (It is exactly because they have created that universe, and are themselves now defined by it or, as we have called it, embedded in it, that they cannot at this point see this similarity. They would have to be able to step mentally outside their universe to see that they are all arguing from a viewpoint based on institutional commitments. And since they cannot step outside that universe except through a transformation that would carry them to a further stage of moral thinking, they cannot now see that they and their opponents share a common foundation of assumptions within which they argue.)

The Structure of Development: A Review

These stages of moral thinking may be the clearest examples of the psychostructural way of understanding our development. We make moral decisions every day, and we are affected by the decisions that children of various ages and other adults make. Thus we pay considerable attention to moral choices, although usually more to their content than to the reasoning that supports that content. So this may be a good place to review some things about how stages and transforming transitions seem to work.

Take first the idea that stages are distinct, and that we grow through them in a fixed order, usually without an ability to return. The dinner guests know one another; they would think George had taken leave of his senses (or had too much to drink) if he suddenly shifted away from arguing on principles of social order as the responsible husband and father and employee he is (responsibilities he shoulders out of stage four duty to institutions), to arguing that executions are good because they make him happy (stage one egocentric pleasure/pain). We can see from our assumptions about how others will act that we do not expect people to return to earlier stages of moral development, even though we do not often think explicitly in these terms.

The Structure of Stage Development

- Everyone begins at the same first stage
- We progress through stages in a fixed order
- We do not ordinarily return to previous stages
- We may pause at an intermediate stage
- We progress from stage to stage through a type-two, transformational change

Notice next that we have some difficulty understanding appreciatively stages we have left behind—Eddie and his teammates will have short patience for a team member who does not do his fair share, but who needs the threat of punishment in order to play his part. Arguments or choices justified by earlier stages of moral reasoning will, if they lead to conclusions of which we do not approve, be condemned as badly reasoned as well as wrong in content.

And notice that while the stage shifts may be imperceptible to the person involved (and are certainly not planned and chosen), they have a transforming quality on the person's moral reasoning. Stage three concern for kinship, duty, and role is not just more of stage two fairness: It is different, although there is an undeniable reasonableness to the progression from one stage to the next when we study it and observe it from the outside.

From the outside we are also able to see something that it may now be time to address. So far we have resisted calling some choices made from the perspective of early stages "mistakes," so that such a judgment would not stand in the way of our understanding. We now know enough to realize that judgments with which we differ can seem correct or even inevitable within the understanding of the person making the judgment—which is, after all, the only way in which she can decide a question at all. With this in mind, we can now afford to look at the limitations that inevitably accompany our partial perceptions at each stage.

The Limitations of Early Stages of Development

For stage one egocentric reward/punishment the limitations are easy enough to see. From our perspective beyond that stage, we observe that it ignores the needs, wants, or even existence of other people except insofar as they are potential sources of reward or punishment. But even within the experience of stage one, the person living at that level will experience more limitations than just occasional punishment. Because the world in fact includes other people with their own desires, reasoning from within stage one will be a poor predictor of the likely outcomes of one's choices (as Eddie's cheating teammate discovered). The person in stage one will find it discomforting; he will see examples of others making decisions that seem to predict consequences more accurately (such as fair trades among the team); and there may be conversation—even the angry objection "You can't do that; it isn't fair!"—that will spur development.

Stage two fairness also suffers from limitations clear to us; life is more complicated than short-range negotiations can account for. But over time the person whose world is at stage two will discover the limits of daily bargaining. Reliable expectations of other people's behavior demand that the child begin to see others, and herself in relationship to them, in stable roles: parent-child, teacher-student, and the like. This both saves the child time and energy, and produces the successful outcomes that are more likely within a more predictable environment.

But stage three interpersonal conformity is not without its own limits. A person at stage three is at the mercy of the biases and blind spots of his group (since he has no way to step outside it and evaluate its values). Thus choices that are at root cultural or esthetic are often called ethical choices by people at this stage. (A good example would be the moral condemnation sometimes expressed by people at stage three for those who do not dress in the conventional way for social activities like churchgoing.) And when two groups made up of members at stage three meet each other, each is convinced of its own rightness and, when they disagree, of the other's wrongness. There is no way for each to step outside of its embeddedness in its own culture to sort out and evaluate differences.

So is stage four the marker of full maturity in moral decision-making? Are George and Martha and Sharon and Frank, having constructed a world of meaning based on social structures and institutions that they sustain unthinkingly and that invisibly sustain them, at the summit? Are the impasse to which they have come in their discussion, and the similar impasses that appear so often between groups and cultures, something for which there is no solution? It is time to look at George's discomfort with Michelle's comment about the relativity of all societies and their laws.

Questions for Reflection and Discussion

1. Recall a public controversy. Stepping beyond the content of each side's argument, what can you see about the manner in which the argument is made? What sorts of motives does the argument at root appeal to? What stage of moral reasoning seems to be at work in making the argument?
2. Consider an issue about which you yourself feel strongly. Try to step outside the content and ask what sort of reasoning you use to support your position. What stage of moral reasoning seems to be at work?
3. What feelings are connected with the attempt to step away from the content of a moral argument which means a great deal to you, so that you can look at the manner of making the judgment instead? What makes this hard to do? What might make it easier?

FOUR

❧

Postconventional Moral Reasoning

During the Vietnam War George's older brother Ernie had opposed American involvement so strongly that he had moved to Canada to avoid the draft. It caused a tremendous row with George's parents, although George—who was only ten—found it difficult to understand either his parents or his brother at the time. Although the war is now a decades-old memory, a similar struggle for understanding had been set into motion within George by Michelle's comment about moral values that have a foundation beyond one's culture and legal system.

By the environment they create and the sanctions they impose for deviance, societies encourage their members to live at the conventional level of moral reasoning (Kohlberg's stages three and four). But society is not a thing different from the collective choices of its members. That most adult choice-makers are at stage three and stage four shapes the expectation that they as a collective—"society"—are set for full adult membership. Thus while we almost never directly think about it in these terms, with reflection we can see that young people are helped to grow through their earlier stages of moral reasoning, and that adults who have failed to do so experience sanctions that range from disapproval to imprisonment. Adults who do not live in the mental world of conventional moral reasoning can expect to be held in suspicion for some of their choices.

Thus George's brother Ernie felt the wrath not only of his draft board but of his parents and his parents' friends when he announced that society's law was not in this case binding on him. His claim to be following a higher standard than legal duty made some people uneasy and most furious. His and George's father, a man who truly loved his children, was distraught at the choice he faced. He would have either to reject his son the "draft-dodger," or overturn (at least in his mind) all that he had worked to create: a society formed and stabilized by socially approved and legally enacted standards. (Of course George's father, embedded in his way of seeing society, could not step outside his worldview to describe it this way; but that in no way lessened his anguish at the choice he faced.)

Again we need to observe here that the direction of Ernie's choice—to disobey society's law in the name of a higher value—was only a part of the reason for the uproar around his decisions. Had he volunteered for military service claiming a higher duty to work for the betterment of humankind by fighting in Vietnam, his decision might have been applauded—but met with equal puzzlement. Ernie was in conflict with his culture not only because of the content of his choice (although the direction in which that choice sent him added to the pain), but because he had developed beyond stage four conventional decision-making. Ernie was undermining the foundations of the way his parents and their peers constructed their moral world.

Many called Ernie a coward. Others claimed he was rationalizing his fear of leaving his friends and his girlfriend. We can note in these accusations that Ernie was being accused of making his decision in ways that his accusers had left behind—stage one or stage three choicemaking. What those who condemned him could not understand was that his basis was something beyond their present ability to comprehend—a way of moral choicemaking that puts even society and its laws under the judgment of a more comprehensive view. Ernie's choice would, through the discomfort it caused some people, encourage them to take a step toward a new level themselves; but most would find the possibility of stepping outside their society's consensus too threatening to contemplate.

We should take stock here. Looking at moral thinking (or any aspect of developmental thinking) from the outside, as we do here, can give us a false sense of superiority. We see clearly what those embedded in choicemaking cannot see at all, exactly because they are embedded in their particular stage of development. Development itself is, in a sense, the progressive ability to step outside what had been one's world and to evaluate that perspective "from outside." But the only "outside" any of us has is some new perspective, some more encompassing worldview. Since the act of reading about worldviews gives us a bit of an opportunity to see each of them from the outside, we run a risk: We can forget that each of us is immersed in a perspective which is so much ours that we cannot see it. We even read the descriptions of perspectives through these lenses of our own worldview, subtly (but to us invisibly) distorting what we read to make it fit comfortably within our world. This is especially a problem as we approach levels of development more encompassing than the conventional, since we may be trying to understand a perspective that is not yet our own. On the other hand, the very act of study may in a slight way encourage us to step outside our present perspective, and to begin to explore the possibility of a larger world. This is usually uncomfortable; sometimes it evokes rage. And just this discomfort was what George was experiencing as he thought about Michelle's comment.

Leaving Conventional-Level Reasoning Behind

If we could have entered Michelle's mind as she commented that society's laws might not be the final word, we would have found that she was herself unsure. She knew that she had begun to consider "society" in a way larger than what she heard from her dinner companions. It encompassed not just the laws of one state today but the wisdom of ages past and of modern sages as well. But the question she felt and asked was even more radical: She was asking whether all law might be only an approximation to something larger and more fundamental, some universal values that, should they come into conflict with a particular law, should override it. She did not know how to sort out such possible conflicts in her own mind, but the possibility bothered her enough that she had to raise the question for her guests.

Postconventional Moral Reasoning: Toward Universals

From Kohlberg's point of view Michelle is entering *stage five* moral thinking. George's brother Ernie had relied on it when he left for Canada. This stage is sometimes called a "prior-to-society" perspective. People choosing from within this view understand that laws and social arrangements are usually legitimate because they reflect genuine values that undergird them; but laws and social contracts do not themselves create or define right and wrong. And if laws or social patterns violate those underlying values, then one's obligation is to the value, not to the law. (You may remember a famous exchange that took place on the floor of the United States Senate on February 29, 1872; in response to a senator from Wisconsin saying, "My country, right or wrong!" Senator Carl Schurz of Missouri replied, "My country, right or wrong; if right, to be kept right; and if wrong, to be set right." This may be an example of the contrast between stage four and stage five thinking; for how can one know one's country needs to be set right unless there is some larger perspective from which to judge its present rightness or wrongness?)

Michelle's uneasiness with her comment differs from George's discomfort with it. His stage four understanding is being challenged. Michelle is beginning to see law and custom and society as if from the outside—a standpoint that George cannot yet take because he cannot find such a perspective. So Michelle's comment strains his ability to understand. But if George is ever to develop to stage five moral thinking, it will be challenges like Michelle's, as well as times that stage four thinking seems to get him into irreconcilable conflicts (perhaps as he looks back and tries to understand the conflict between his father and his older brother), that will lead him there. The prescriptions of his religious faith might also be of help: for while George has to this point comfortably understood the biblical phrase "we must obey God rather than men" (Acts 5:29b) by identifying the civil society and its laws with God's will, the phrase is open to another interpretation which would subvert his stage four way of thinking.

For Michelle the confusion is different. She has moved to an appreciation of values that are prior to law. But she knows that law and values sometimes conflict, and is uncomfortable with the tension between them. If she eventually comes to be able to see this conflict as if from outside, rather than being embedded in it, she will have come to Kohlberg's *stage six*, a morality based on universal principles personally embraced, with a commitment to those principles and to law and social custom only insofar as they embody those principles. Michelle is not at that point as she makes her observation about society's limits in the after-dinner conversation. But enough conversations like this, and perhaps opportunities to be influenced by the writings or presence of others who do reason at stage six, might help her toward that reconciliation of law and principle.

The Context and Structure of Transformational Change

Before we leave aside Kohlberg's work we should look again at what we have seen here about how people change. The basic structure of transformation outlined by Haughton (chapter 1) can be made a bit more specific now. We can see what sort of environment encourages development (here, to postconventional moral decision-making). American society remembers and honors (even if often not fully understanding) incidents such as Senator Schurz's Senate reply, and the biblical sayings, and the literature that tells of moral geniuses such as Mohandas Gandhi and Aleksandr Solzhenitsyn and the Reverend Martin Luther King, Jr. Interested individuals who have discovered the limits of conventional (stages three and four) decision-making can find serious literature and serious discussion that might create a "weak spot." (Totalitarian and closed societies can make moral development more rare through censorship, depriving people of such provocations—something we might remember when provoked by protest movements in our own culture.) And the freedoms our society guarantees allow persons making decisions at the postconventional level some latitude to criticize publicly society's laws and customs, so there is always the opportunity to find at least a small community of people whose manner of moral reasoning—whether or not we agree with their conclusions—is at a postconventional level.

But a caution is also necessary here. Not every criticism of law and custom is made from a postconventional perspective, even if that is the language used. Groups and individuals can adopt the language of "principles" and "values" but use it to support conclusions they have already settled on from other motives, which may be conventional or even preconventional. To oppose a war, say, might truly be motivated by self-interest or by the opinions of one's group, and be described in a lofty rhetoric of principle because such language is convenient, flattering, and confirming of one's rightness. And no matter what stage of moral reasoning one has arrived at, wrong decisions are always possible because of bad information, weakness of will, or evil intent. Vigorous debate—in society, church, neighborhood, and family—is vital for good decision-making. An appreciation of moral reasoning and its stages of development does not spare us careful inquiry and disciplined thinking. But it may make us cautious in dismissing others' judgments and more careful to engage in civil and genuine dialogue with those with whom we disagree. We can become aware that our own and others' conclusions may be inadequate because of the limitations of perspective that come with preconventional and conventional stages, as well as from illusion and wickedness that can corrupt judgment at any stage.

The structure of stages and transformations between stages, first developed by Piaget in work with children and extended to adult moral decision-making by Kohlberg and others, has also been expanded to encompass more comprehensive attitudes to life and ways of living. We look next at research on what may seem farthest from the domain of psychology, the development of faith.

Questions for
Reflection and Discussion

1. Think of some recent controversies in which people have disobeyed the civil law in the name of a higher law: How did these play out? What feelings did they evoke in you? What can you now see about how stages of moral reasoning might have played a part in each controversy?

2. What forces or elements in our culture encourage the growth of moral reasoning to postconventional levels? What pressures discourage such growth? Can you locate similar aids and pressures in the church, or in other groups you may be involved in?

3. Thinking of your personal history, what events, people, circumstances, or challenges can you locate that might have encouraged or discouraged your own development in this area of moral reasoning?

FIVE

⊘

Growing in Faith

It was a night several weeks after their dinner party, and Tim and Michelle were in bed talking about their son. Eddie had recently started his formal religious education at their church, and Tim was not happy with what Eddie was hearing and doing there. Tim's own parents, although lovers of literature who shared their enthusiasm with him, had avoided all formal religion. Tim's exposure began when he had followed his girlfriend away to college, to a school sponsored by a Christian denomination. There he had become absorbed in courses on the Bible and theology and was an active member of a student Christian group. What was presented in those classes made sense to Tim, who was studying to become an engineer. The Bible was full of facts; theology made connections among those facts; those connections showed the way one should live; and the church group provided a fellowship that supported that way of life. Looking back on what he considered his own religiously wasted childhood years, Tim wanted something different for Eddie. He wanted religious information, and lots of it, for his son. But the classes at their church did not seem to have too much of that.

Certainly Eddie was hearing stories from the Bible; but he was coming home with pictures he had drawn of the Bible characters, not lessons to study. He was learning his prayers (prayers Michelle and Tim had already been teaching him), but

51

Tim did not find that there was enough content in the lessons. And he had trouble understanding what the program's director had told him: that Eddie was at a stage in his life at which the stories and their drama would influence Eddie and his peers more strongly than the facts and arguments that had so captured Tim's imagination in college.

Research on Faith Development

The person to whom we can turn in order to understand both Eddie's lessons and Tim's concern is James Fowler (b. 1940). Influenced by Erikson and Piaget and especially by Kohlberg, Fowler set out beginning in the 1970s to see whether that elusive but powerful part of ourselves we call *faith* developed in the way that thinking and moral reasoning did. Looking at the formal structures of faith (the "how") rather than the contents of particular beliefs (religious or not, the "what"), Fowler and his colleagues uncovered and described a progression through six stages. As in the work of Piaget and Kohlberg, it seems that the stages appear in a fixed order, that one cannot skip over steps, that not a few people remain at earlier stages even throughout adulthood, and that the spur to movement from stage to stage comes both from outside (in the form of people and ideas reflecting higher stage development) and from within (because each earlier stage has inadequacies). In short, faith development seems to fit a general constructive-developmental model. But we need to be clear that persons do not grow in lockstep: one's cognitive, moral, and faith development can be at different stages (although it appears that sometimes a particular level of cognitive development has to be reached before a certain stage of faith development can occur).

So we can look at Tim's uncertainty and at Eddie's education through the lens of Fowler's work, summarized in Table 2.[1]

Table 2. Stages of Faith Development

Name	Stage	Characterized by:
Undifferentiated	0	Experiences of a trustworthy or threatening environment
Intuitive-projective	1	Moods, images, story elements, fantasy
Mythic-literal	2	Stories and rituals of belonging to a community
Synthetic-conventional	3	Shaping of a unified sense of self in world
Individuative-reflective	4	Self-aware decision to take responsibility for one's outlook
Conjunctive	5	Attempts to reconcile apparent opposites such as logic and myth
Universalizing	6	Selfless work to transform the world; sense of universal community

The Foundations of Faith

Eddie's education in faith began long before formal schooling, as did Tim's and Michelle's, and as did yours and mine. The foundation of faith is, for good or ill, laid in infancy. Love and protection received from others plant the seeds of courage; neglect and abandonment, the opposite. Interacting with his or her parents lays groundwork in every infant for a sense of mutuality and trust, or for one of fear and self-protection. Fowler admits that this stage is largely impossible to research in a conventional way, but the consequences of early infant experience color all that follows. Fowler calls this time of infancy a pre-stage, undifferentiated faith. Tim's parents may have avoided all formal religion, but they were giving Tim his first exposure to the world of faith in the way they cared for him. Tim's college experience shows that there had been strengths in that care; but his lack of religious training also left him with burdens, as we shall see.

Eddie's training in his classes is designed to fit Fowler's stage one, *intuitive-projective faith*. Young children (Fowler says typically ages 3–7) develop in faith largely through their imaginations. Images, stories, experiences, and other surprising novelties come from parents and others close to the child; and Eddie's life at this stage is guided largely by his perceptions, so he is an eager recipient. Eddie will also begin to take note during these years of the human realities of sex and death, and of the cultural taboos and emotions around them. He will not understand these things, of course, but the tone of adults' feelings will linger in him. Eddie will not put these images and feelings into any coherent story until a further stage, but the fragmented parts now engage him not so much on the level of thought as through his moods and feelings and affections. Eddie will be a sponge for the emotional climate of his home, his classroom, and his culture. And of course he is not at all yet capable of absorbing even in a simplified way the sorts of material that so engaged Tim in college.

But Eddie's next stage of development will bring him a major step toward coherence, if not critical thinking. Fowler's stage two is called *mythic-literal faith*, because stories are at the heart of it. In a few years Eddie will be captivated by myths and other narratives, from *Star Wars* movies and *Harry Potter* books to tales of King David and of Jesus. Missing the stories of this religious kind in his own youth is what gives rise to Tim's concern for Eddie. Looking back, Tim is aware that he missed out on a treasure of religious information and symbolism during his own childhood and had to compensate for that later. But Tim clearly did use the literary and other materials available to him from his parents and school to navigate into and beyond this stage of faith himself.

Again, the stages of faith are marked out not by *what* we believe, but *how* we believe. Children at the mythic-literal (stage two) level use whatever materials they can find to make a coherent story out of their lives. If the materials they rely on contain symbolic elements, the child will take them literally; gods and heroes will be imagined with very human attributes. At this stage children are embedded in their stories; they cannot step out of them to analyze or criticize through conceptual reasoning.

Faith That Makes Sense of Life with Others

And even at Fowler's next stage, stage three *synthetic-conventional faith*, reasoning will not play a central role. This stage is the province of adolescents who have now grown beyond stage two (and also, Fowler says, of many adults; it is not unusual for adults to remain at stage three). Stage three faith is rooted in an awareness of our life with others. The family is no longer the only world of the person; now there are friends, school or work, and the wider society. The job of faith at this stage is to make coherent sense of these multiple demands and interests. Faith must tell me who I am (a question of *identity*), and how I properly fit and interact (a question of what Fowler calls *outlook*).

It is not hard to observe stage three, since many adults display it. Faith at this stage gives one a way to weave disparate experiences into a unity; it provides a platform for moral values and for beliefs about oneself, others, and the world. The very sincerity and conviction with which such beliefs are held, and the way in which others may be evaluated in terms of their conformity to these beliefs, are signs of such a person's embeddedness in this perspective. One at this stage cannot step outside it to evaluate and criticize. (There is a bumper sticker that reads, "God said it. I believe it. That ends it." The saying is a perfect description of stage three faith.)

We might take note here of the various "fundamentalisms" of today's world. Stage three faith, with its one-sided confidence in clarity and certainty, can provide a foundation on which experiences of exploitation or other grievances can build. Our developmental perspective can help us to understand the temptation to fundamentalism (of scriptural interpretation, or church dogma, or cultural values, or patriotism, or revolutionary creed); the limitations of the fundamentalist viewpoint; and a potential path beyond such rigidity.[2] What people with a fundamentalist approach to their faith believe surely matters; but the way in which people hold their beliefs—that is, their stage of faith development—matters as well. It is surely not true that people at stage three are budding fundamentalists; but fundamentalism of some sort may well be at least a temptation when people at this stage are under stress. The rising popularity of fundamentalist churches in our culture, and the increasing power of scriptural or dogmatic fundamentalism in mainstream churches, show that people in our own culture are not exempt from this temptation. We can appreciate the role that faith development plays in this cultural drama by looking at stage three faith's strengths and weaknesses, and at the path beyond it.

Stage three faith has many virtues; the world is complicated and disparate, and faith now unifies those pressures and gives a sense of identity. But stage three faith and having one's own distinct identity do not sit comfortably together, for stage three cannot encompass a truly distinctive self. Identity at stage three is built on meeting the expectations of the other people whom one values, and on conforming to the dictates of one's social group, religious organization, and institutional authorities. A foundation built on personal autonomy to evaluate such commitments will have to wait for development into stage four, which is where we find Tim when we look back to his college years.

Faith That Honors Individuality

Arriving at college Tim was the product of his excellent family and education; he fit into his surroundings well, and he found that his society's expectations fit him comfortably. He was sensitive to the signals of approval from others, dedicated himself to what was defined as achievement, and understood himself through the lens of the literature he had come to love and the values he had grown up with and which he had come to imitate. Tim was comfortably secure at stage three—except for the apparent oddity of his girlfriend's religious devotion. Michelle would cause Tim to

leave home in more than a geographical sense when he followed her away to college.

In the college classroom Tim was challenged to step
away from what he had come to assume. His professors
raised questions about how his ethnicity, his economic sta-
tus, his gender, his social class, his citizenship, and his religion (in Tim's case, nonreligion) could be justified. He was
asked to learn to be critical; to look for evidence, for incon-
sistencies, and for self-interest in what until that moment he
had taken for granted as natural and inevitable, at least for
people of his sort. These forces were encouraging Tim to step
outside his embeddedness in his previous home and culture.
In the course of learning what in his background to retain
and what to put aside, he discovered a foundation for his
identity that was truly chosen in a way it had not been until
this point. And then there was Michelle.

Their bond was a great source of encouragement for
Tim, and her own faith was a challenge to him. But her religious conviction did not sit well with Tim's parents, and in
following her to her college Tim had had to reject his parents' wishes and advice. While the break was civil and cour-
teous, it nonetheless marked a shift in Tim's sense of himself.
The move, and later his and Michelle's decision to marry,
had set him on a course from which he could turn back only
at a cost. He had made decisions which could not be unmade.
And as the awareness that there are such choices in life
became a part of his outlook, he moved toward Fowler's
stage four, *individuative-reflective faith*.

Fowler's title is carefully chosen, and we see each part
of it in Tim's experience. For the first time, as he steps away
from the taken-for-granted values and patterns of his
upbringing, he has the opportunity to create a self-chosen set
of commitments. He is now fashioning an identity and an
outlook that are fundamentally his own, not unwitting bor-

rowings from his upbringing. He is becoming an individual, as distinct from simply one of a group. And he is choosing among values and commitments because he can look at them with an outsider's perspective, no longer embedded in the world that he had taken as given.

Thus faith at this stage is *individuative*: It creates an individual. And faith at this stage is also *reflective*: The creation of an individual self comes about by awareness and choice. Tim's development to this stage allowed him to choose to embrace a religious way of life different from the pattern of his upbringing. He chose it in no small part because the style of critical thinking that he found in his theology classes was well-matched to the developmental stage in which he was becoming at home. And of course the example of Michelle provoked him to imagine a new possibility. But note that he did not embrace religion on account of Michelle, to be like her because he valued her; that would be typical of stage three. But while Tim may have at first left for college with her on that basis—and "leaving home" (physically and/or emotionally) is acknowledged by Fowler as a frequent spur to stage three–four transition—so now she provided a different sort of challenge. Her religious commitment did not fit into Tim's world; the quest to find a place for such commitment led him to question the foundations of that world he had thus far created. And his quest led him, after a struggle, to his new sense of himself within a new and larger world.

> *"Leaving home" (physically and/or emotionally) is a frequent spur to stage three–four transition.*

Stages of Faith: How We Believe, Not What We Believe

We should note here that two shifts have happened in Tim's life. While he may see the change from being nonreligious to being religious as the more dramatic, he has also undergone a significant change in how he believes. Again we need to separate the *content* (Tim's formerly nonreligious, and now religious, convictions) from the *structure* (the way in which Tim holds those convictions). The language here is important: Fowler would call the change in content a "conversion"—a dramatic reordering of the content of belief. We need to distinguish this from the new way in which Tim has come to hold his beliefs, for the new structure marks a type-two change in stage, a transformation of his *way* of believing. Our story has the two shifts happen to Tim at the same time, but they need not. A person might undergo conversion (change in content of belief) at any stage; and Tim or anyone might grow from stage three to stage four faith without any shift in content, for the transformation in stage describes how the beliefs are held, not what those beliefs are in themselves.

Tim as we meet him today is comfortably in stage four. The conceptual, rational approach to faith has been both a comfort and a prod to him through the years. He understands the mythic and symbolic features of his belief by translating them for himself into rational terms; he "sees through" the rituals to their meanings; and it is his very comfort with this rationality in his faith that makes Eddie's pictures of biblical characters so disturbing. But to understand *why* he is now talking with Michelle about that, we need to turn to Fowler's understanding of the next step in faith development, stage five *conjunctive faith*.

Later Stages of Faith: Recapturing What Was Good in the Past in a New Way

Stage four faith is a significant accomplishment; through rational critique it is able to gain some distance on religious imagery, symbolism, creeds, and organizations so as to evaluate and understand them. But in gaining critical distance it also deprives the person at stage four of some of the richness that is carried in the more-than-rational aspects of myth, symbol, and ritual. Faith at its best opens us to the wonder and terror of an unimaginably vast cosmos. Sacred traditions have long understood that the poetry of symbol and ritual is a more adequate vehicle to convey wonder and terror than is the prose of paragraphs and definitions (however necessary those are in their proper place). Eddie's childish drawings are making Tim vaguely aware that he is missing out on the poetry of faith through his embeddedness in its prose.

We must be careful here. Earlier stages of development, especially Fowler's stages two and three, might be described as poetic in one sense, for they do not involve critical distancing from one's commitments and have a lively awareness of symbol (to the point of being embedded in it). Tim could mistakenly attribute his dissatisfaction with the distancing of stage four faith to a nostalgic desire to return to what might seem an easier way of believing at stage two or three. But the impetus to growth is not that; it is to a new stage in which Tim will step out of his embeddedness in rationality and see things from a larger perspective in which he will not lose what he has attained through the prose of reason. In stage five he will add and integrate the poetry which captures the music as well as the words of faith.

Stage five conjunctive faith is rare, Fowler says, before midlife. Developing into it will require of Tim that he soften the hard edges of rationality—not to abandon it, but to see its limitations. He will have to admit that paradoxes sometimes capture reality more adequately than definitions. And in the personal realm he will have to learn that there are springs of wisdom within him that arise from the symbol-making power of his own unconscious self. As he deals with others he will have to learn to appreciate differences as often-helpful multiple perspectives on a truth larger than any one individual or culture can grasp. He will have to learn to seek out such differences, so that they can be put into conversation with his own perspective. He will have to learn to see in Eddie's drawings a sort of window into his former self and into the mystery beyond every self. As he wrestles with his discomfort in conversation with Michelle, he may come to take these steps. Or he may find a way to put aside his discomfort and to live for a few more years or decades in the equilibrium that stage four offers.

Universalizing Faith and Religious Genius

While we may occasionally have contact with someone whose faith is at stage five, Fowler proposes a further stage that he himself admits is exceedingly rare. We see it in the well-known and revered (and usually deceased) prophets and religious geniuses of all ages and cultures, and perhaps in a very few obscure but magnetic contemporaries. Fowler describes this stage six faith as having passed beyond boundaries of culture, ethnicity, class, and all the rest, to allow such a person to embody in her or his particular way the transcendent. Thus he calls stage six *universalizing* faith. He also mentions that such people frequently suffer martyrdom at the hands of their contemporaries because their appeal to universal values is, despite its appeal, such a subversive threat to every culture. We might imagine historical figures such as the Buddha, or near contemporaries like Blessed Mother Teresa, Pope John Paul II, and Thomas Merton, as giving at least some intimation of what such faith might be like.

As Tim and Michelle discuss Tim's concern with Eddie's education and—although unwittingly—challenge Tim to grow to a new stage in his own faith, we can see the natural progression of our own development. Researchers focus on particular aspects of our lives, and we have traced the findings of developmental studies in thinking (with Piaget), in moral decision-making (with Kohlberg) and now in faith. And there is still another aspect of development that the entire conversation here takes for granted; for Tim and Michelle are talking as spouses, and about their child. The stage is set to look at the way we develop as embodied, sexual women and men.

Questions for Reflection and Discussion

1. Has there been an occasion in your life in which you "left home" in the sense of letting go of a former way of believing? How would you describe that experience in the light of this chapter's explanation of faith stages?

2. What stage do you think is most widely represented in the way religious faith is talked about in the mass media? What brings you to this conclusion? What stage of faith do you find most frequently encouraged in sermons, homilies, or classes in your church congregation?

3. In your experience what has helped you in making transitions to more developed stages of faith? Can you recall the feelings that accompanied one or more of those transitions?

Six

Psychosexual Development

"Grandma, do you have a 'gina like I do and like Mommy does?" Amanda's opening conversational gambit when Michelle took the children to visit her mother Pauline was certainly startling. But we have come far enough in understanding development to suspect that we should put our detective skills to work here. What sort of world is Amanda living in that makes this question interesting to her? Earlier in her life she would not have known to ask, nor would she care; in a few years she will not need to ask. But the process of which we catch a glimpse here is not simply a matter of her adding facts to her knowledge of biology (although sex education is sometimes wrongly reduced to that). Amanda is, like every child and every adult, on the path of what researchers have come to call *psychosexual development*.

Our understanding of this aspect of our journey, at least as we are now equipped to explore and describe it, is somewhat different from the cognitive and moral and faith development theories of the previous chapters. For one thing, careful constructive-developmental research on psychosexual development is largely undone. For another, in this aspect of our lives we have physical markers of different stages as well as social and cultural rituals that surround such events as puberty, parenthood, and menopause. So rather than following a path that pays attention primarily to the inner experiences of embeddedness and transformation as we have done previously, in this area we can to some degree connect our appreciation of the developing person's inner world to changes and experiences that an outside observer can see. But the focus will still be primarily on the inner world of a person's experience and understanding. We will try to understand what we see from the outside as clues to, and sometimes consequences of, that inner world of the developing person.

A Model for Psychosexual Development

Here it will be helpful to use a descriptive model taken from Michael Cavanagh.[1] He uses the conventional three stages of sexual life (childhood, adolescence, and adulthood), and divides each into phases, three for childhood (four if prenatal experience is counted separately), three for adolescence, and two for adulthood. (See Table 3.)[2]

Table 3. Stages of Psychosexual Development

Stage	*Phase*	*Described as:*
I: Childhood sexuality	1	Sexual unawareness
	2	Sexual awakening
	3	Sexual surreptitiousness
II: Adolescent sexuality	1	Sexual fantasy
	2	Sexual preoccupation
	3	Superficial sexual relating
III: Adult sexuality	1	Psychosexual mutuality
	2	Psychosexual integration

But as with other aspects of our survey, it would be a mistake to focus too much on chronological age or even physical changes; what matters most is the inner understanding and perception, and the choices that flow from them.

Childhood Sexuality: A Focus on the Self

We should start at the beginning. A few years before the visit to Grandma Pauline, when Amanda was still in Michelle's womb, she was a sexual person—though of course unaware of it. Not only was she at that point a very little girl, but she was also occasionally experiencing what she would much later come to know as the signs of sexual arousal. Lubrication of her vagina would take place, just as a few years earlier her brother Eddie had experienced erections while still in Michelle's womb. Much of the process of Amanda's lifelong psychosexual development would be her making of connections: between on the one hand what is given by nature, her bodily and emotional experiences; and on the other her awareness of their significance and possibilities to herself and, potentially, to others.

It may be worthwhile to pause here and pay more attention to these connections, for making them well is at the heart of proper psychosexual development and most likely also at the core of living a virtuous and happy sexual life. One part of our sexual development is given to us: Our bodies mature without need for our conscious assistance. And yet our maturing bodies pose a series of questions to our awareness: "What is it to be a woman or a man?" "How do I relate appropriately to others as the sexual person I am and that each of them is?" "What does the capacity of my sexuality to bring new life mean about how I should properly think about myself and my relationships?" "How do I do justice to myself and to others in the choices I make?" "How do I come to terms with the experiences I have along the way?" Guidance in answering these questions will come from a variety of sources outside ourselves; some of it will be true wisdom, some limited by cultural blindnesses, and perhaps some useless or even destructive. But the heart of the matter is the shaping of one's own imagination, perceptions, understanding, decisions, values, and habits. Psychosexual development theory is the mapping of the typical stages of how we make those connections between what is given by our embodiment and what is created by our awareness.

To make it easier to say clearly what one is talking about in this realm, a convention of language has become popular: Many writers will use *sexuality* to refer to the entire experience of embodied living as male or female, including but going far beyond what the word *sex* is often taken to mean. The experiences of sexual arousal, intimacy, and orgasm are described more specifically with the word *genitality*. This book will use that convention, although readers should be aware that it is not universal. Some authors also use the words *sex* and *gender* in specific ways, but the distinction between *sexuality* and *genitality* is enough for us here. So if you were surprised to hear of infants experiencing erections or lubrications before birth, you were working under the common and correct assumption that *sexuality* is a feature of infant life, for you knew that each infant is a girl or boy. But you were surprised to hear that *genitality* is also a feature of prenatal life if you did not already know that arousal is experienced in the womb.

Sexuality and Genitality

- *Sexuality refers to our embodied life as women or men*

- *Genitality refers to experiences of arousal, physical intimacy, and orgasm*

Before her birth and for some time after it Amanda was discovering her body and her world. (You may remember that in Piaget's sensorimotor stage infants "learn by doing.") So just as she learned by experiment that she could remove her sock but not her foot, she also discovered about her body that certain experiences (such as rubbing her genitals) could give her pleasure. This natural, normal, and necessary exploration is the foundation for later adult experience and relationships. Childhood sexuality and genitality are an awakening to oneself.

The first phase of stage one *childhood sexuality* is called *sexual unawareness* by Cavanagh. But we should not think that means that little Amanda (and you and I) were not conscious of our bodies and the experiences we had in them. Touch—of skin against womb, then later of mouth to breast and tiny hand to skin—tells the infant a great deal about the world. Michelle and Tim handled baby Amanda gently and often; they encouraged her to explore herself and her world in every safe way; and as a result Amanda developed a sense that it was a *good* thing to live in her body, and her body became a source of confidence and joy. The "unawareness" of which Cavanagh speaks refers to the infant's inability to name or think about these experiences; she is embedded in them, to use Kegan's term. What is being laid down in memory is more a foundation of emotion and feeling than of conscious thought. But at tea with Grandma Pauline little Amanda was well beyond that.

Phase two of childhood sexuality is called *sexual awakening*: in it Amanda is becoming conscious of being embodied. From infancy to toddlerhood multiple things have been happening in her: She has learned to speak, become toilet trained, and right now is doing her best to understand, with grandma's startled help, her similarity to other "girls" and their difference from "boys." She is discovering her own sexual identity. This unself-conscious curiosity can be disarming to adults who may not understand it. Children at this stage will walk into the living room naked without a thought, no matter who happens to be visiting. They ask questions as the questions arise to them. Adults who can respond without anxiety help the child along the way. Discomfort among adults at childhood spontaneity is usually expressed in teasing, embarrassed giggling, or, worse, shaming; and it passes adult discomfort on to the child in a lesson of shame and fear. Michelle will properly start to teach Amanda that there are times and places for nakedness, and that there are conventions to be observed in conversation; but the important and fundamental lesson Amanda needs to learn is that her bodily and sexual life and her curiosity are all good gifts. Such a lesson will make her properly adventurous as she grows into the final childhood stage, phase three *sexual surreptitiousness.*

Even children with the very best of parents, since they are growing up in a society tremendously uncomfortable with children's sexuality, will become somewhat discreet after the directness about sexuality that marked phase two. That new-found discretion might lead parents who have a vague memory of Freud's theory of a latency period to relax into the hope that middle and later childhood will be a respite before the turmoil of the teen years. And children in phase three do seem to lose interest in sex in general and in sexual differences in particular. But the key word here is *seem.* Their sexuality has taken a turn toward the private. Out of sight of adults there is an increasing interest in sexual material, sexual play, self-pleasuring, and the entire enterprise of continuing discovery. In this phase Amanda will no longer ask her grandmother about sex; but she will be determined to find the answers to questions she continues to have, and to seek to discover whatever she can about this intriguing world—so long as she can do it without unduly disturbing her parents.

The whole of stage one, childhood sexuality, is a time for self-discovery. What separates it from stage two, *adolescent sexuality*, is its focus on the self. While Amanda might well have been involved with other children in games of sexual exploration, those others were in a sense incidental to her own discoveries, not the focus of the experience. This will change in stage two. Marked outwardly by puberty, the inner shift is perhaps more dramatic as a growing teen forges a link between sexual experience and relating to others. To appreciate this we might leave Amanda's story aside for a bit, and turn instead to the teenage years of her father, Tim.

Adolescent Sexuality: Learning about One's Self in Relationship

Tim's venture into sexual relating began long before he met Michelle. It began, in fact, not between him and any middle-school crush, but in his own imagination. Before Tim would experiment with a real relationship he first tried out aspects of such a venture in his mind. Tim built a bridge into relationship through what has given phase one of adolescent psychosexual development its name, *sexual fantasy.*

We might note here that this should not be surprising. Tim had, by his late middle-school years, become adept at thinking things through and planning, at least in the short term. He could envision how the boards of a clubhouse would fit together before starting to assemble them. He was used to arranging things mentally before doing so in the physical world. From our growing understanding of development we might recognize that Tim is by this point cognitively well-established in Piaget's stage of concrete operations, and he may be entering the stage of formal operations with its ability to think abstractly. Tim naturally applied his growing prowess at anticipation to the realm of sexual relationships through fantasy.

So consider Tim now in his early teens. The pressures of hormonal change are affecting both his body and his interests. Along with this, the social climate of his circle of friends and his culture is making it likely that he will experience some romantic attraction—quite possibly idealized and not reciprocated. (We looked briefly at the transformational nature of "falling in love" in chapter 1.) Tim enters stage two psychosexual development, adolescent sexuality, as his interest shifts away from self-understanding toward the possibility of a relationship. And at first he explores this unfamiliar territory in his imagination. He connects childhood's disconnected sexual and genital impulses and insights into a coherent story. He becomes his own author, weaving plots that involve him with others but do not expose his naïveté to possible rejection or even ridicule. Sexual fantasy allows him to explore in safety, and through it he begins to forge a crucial link among his own genital longings, his sense of himself, and other people.

Tim is, of course, developing in all areas of his life; and it will be because of this wider newly developing emotional competence, especially his self-respect and self-direction, that he will slowly begin to experiment with turning his fantasies into reality. So by his middle teens Tim is ready for the second phase of adolescent sexuality, what his parents would come to consider the aptly named phase of *sexual preoccupation*.

These years were the time of Tim's most intense sexual interest. His parents might have called him "girl-crazy," but for Tim the landscape was broader. He was discovering who he was in relationship to real other persons, now not simply as the child of his parents but as a person in his own right. He experimented with attaching himself to this group, then that; became caught up in one fad, then another; changed the style of his hair and clothing with dramatic swiftness; and, of course, began to relate to chosen people in a newly intimate way. He and his sequential girlfriends were engaged in a process of mutual exploration of the roles both of physical intimacy and of emotional revelation in a relationship. He and his peers were discovering what sort of person each was, what they liked and did not like, what they chose to draw toward themselves as an aspect of their maturing identity, and what to leave behind. The intensity of this experience (sometimes called "sexual saturation") allows the developing adolescent eventually to put sexuality into the wider perspective of an integrated adult life of relationship. Learning what role an intimate relationship will play in his life is the business of the third phase in adolescent sexuality. By late in high school Tim was ready for an experience that to him would hardly fit the name given it by Cavanagh. The scholar might have called phase three *superficial sexual relating*; but to Tim it was the time he fell in love with Michelle.

"Superficial" might best be understood in the sense that Tim was, despite the intensity of his feeling for Michelle, still self-centered. Romantic love begins in a feeling of incompleteness and in a hope that someone else can fulfill one and make one whole. This was the psychological energy behind Tim's previous crushes, and even of his enthusiasms for his hobbies. But now, as Tim knows himself better, his sense of what might fulfill him has more distinct lines. The mutuality of his love with Michelle is tremendously affirming, for her acceptance of him (although also somewhat self-centered, though neither knows it) helps him to trust more firmly in the sort of person he is becoming. And their growing emotional and physical intimacy both expresses and propels further risky self-revelation between them. In short, they are growing to be friends as well as romantic partners. The experience of conflict, as they begin to discover their differences and have to learn to find a place in the relationship for difference, will be a vital part of becoming' friends. The deepening of friendship, and the integration of more of each one's sense of self as their self-revelation and mutual acceptance continue to deepen, will bring them over time out of the adolescent stage of development and into adult sexual relating. But that would get us ahead of our story; we should first look at a few of the difficulties that the idealized story of Tim and Michelle has avoided—but that many people in the real world do not.

> *Romantic love begins in a feeling of incomplete-*
> *ness and in a hope that someone else can fulfill the*
> *person and make one whole.*

Difficulties in Psychosexual Development

Tim's story has been full of strengths: both inner ones, to navigate with courage the challenges of moving from phase to phase, and outer ones of a benign and even encouraging family and culture. When these are lacking the step to a next phase may be too much of a challenge for the growing person. And then, just as we have seen with moral development and faith development, a person may find a plateau at some point of growth and remain there. And because psychosexual development plays such a pervasive role in our lives, we may be able to see around us or even in ourselves aspects of unfinished business from this sort of interrupted development.

Disorders that emerge when people in adult bodies still live developmentally in the world of childhood are particularly tragic. If parents or culture fails to foster the embodiment of a very young child with holding and touching and embracing, as well as with the ordinary sorts of care, the child may suffer throughout life with a sense of being somehow wrong and inadequate. He or she may find the entire domain of sexuality uncharted territory, and have only a weak sense of being a sexual person at all, even if married and a parent. In older childhood harsh responses to childhood curiosity may mark the entire area as dangerous territory for the growing child, and lead to a sense in adulthood that one's sexual desires are somehow shameful and abnormal. Adults marooned here will keep their sexual wishes secret even from partners, feeling as though they must keep a secret about their sexuality lest they be exposed and rejected. In the most tragic cases, it may be that continuing and compulsive sexual interest in children, pedophilia, has its roots in failures of psychosexual development at a very early stage.

It seems that failures to grow beyond adolescent phases are more common. A glance at a newsstand or at the Internet will show how much sexual fantasy, from pornography to romance novels to soap opera, pervades the life of many adults. And although sexual preoccupation is technically the name of phase two adolescent sexuality, many would apply it to contemporary culture as a whole. (We should note that sexual preoccupation can also be expressed as a crusade against sexual information and genital pleasure. The antipornography vigilante and the sex addict may have more in common than they know.) The quest for one romantic adventure after another that some call "serial monogamy" is little different from phase three superficial sexual relating—except for the vital difference that it is carried out compulsively, not at its proper time of life, and often leaves untold damage, especially to children, in its wake.

While we can notice and lament such failures to grow, condemnation is hardly helpful. In many cases it was fear, shaming, and rejection that blocked growth in the first place. The wiser first task is to understand, even understand appreciatively, that imperfect people are quite possibly doing what *seems* appropriate within the mental world in which they are embedded. And while society rightly has to protect itself from the damage that damaged people can do, through restricting pedophiles' contact with children and through careful protection of children's needs when parents divorce, the ultimate hope is that the proper sorts of affirmation, support, and guidance can help troubled people to resume the path of development. For some deeply wounded few this may tax the ability of the best therapy; fortunately for most of us opportunity and guidance are offered in everyday living if we are honest and conscientious. And to return to our story, it was exactly the everydayness of a deepening relationship between Michelle and Tim that led them, although after some years of marriage and at different times, into stage three adult psychosexual living.

Adult Sexuality: Seeing Clearly, Giving Generously, Loving Differences

Although marriage is not the only expression of the adult phases (and although most couples entering marriage are probably not yet at this level), the words of the wedding vows express the significant shift between adolescent and adult levels of psychosexual development. Adolescent levels are, at their proper time, appropriately self-interested; they are the path of one's growth in self-understanding. Tim and Michelle's first few years of marriage were still marked by self-interest, as if they heard but could scarcely take to heart that the vows said "for worse...for poorer...in sickness." What each could gain from the marriage held center stage; only slowly would what each could give to the other come to the fore.

Phase one of stage three, *adult sexuality*, is called *psychosexual mutuality*.[3] It is marked by a shift in interest so that the relationship becomes an opportunity to give and to share, more than to receive. Genitality becomes one important but integrated aspect of a wider relationship of care, support, trust, vulnerability, and challenge. This sort of relating is a significant achievement, but partners need to appreciate that it is not the last word. Inevitably, the balance between proper care of oneself and care for another begins as a precarious dance. Necessary discoveries of this phase—that there is more than one valid way to look at things, that some matters can be compromised about and others cannot, that taking responsibility for oneself is a foundation for taking responsibility for others—are at the beginning tentative. The prospect of unending deeper discovery and intimacy is held out by Cavanagh in the open-ended phase two, *psychosexual integration*.[4] We might take Michelle's mother Pauline as an example. Even after the death of her husband her care for her daughter and grandchildren, as well as for the other seniors in her retirement community, is an expression of the compassion and generosity that at this point have become a part of her because of her lifelong psychosexual development.

As we progress through the stages and phases we can note that the distinctive place in life given to sexuality and genitality seems less pronounced. This is not because these are less important, but because they are more thoroughly woven into a person's unique life. As we become more integrated in our impulses, desires, understanding, virtues, and commitments, it becomes more difficult and less necessary to follow a single strand or aspect within the person. The unification of our disparate and sometimes dissonant energies may be a distant goal, but the developing person learns to create a symphony in which each distinctive instrument blends more fully with the others. The work of the next researcher will introduce us to the aspect of ourselves that we might imagine as the symphony's conductor—not playing an instrument, but coordinating them all. The next chapter is dedicated to the work of Jane Loevinger on what is called ego development.

Questions for Reflection and Discussion

1. What sorts of lessons about your own sexuality were you taught as you were growing up? What would you change, if you could? How have those lessons affected your adult life? How do you (or would you) help children and young people today to appreciate their sexuality?
2. What feelings arise as you think or talk about sexuality and genitality? Do you see any connections between these feelings and the way you were raised?
3. Have there been times that your sense of yourself as embodied and sexual underwent a major shift? Can you make connections between them and the outline in this chapter?

SEVEN

Ego Development

We last met Ernie, George's older brother, in chapter four as he fled the Vietnam-era draft to Canada and in doing so revealed the limits of his father's and his culture's stage of moral reasoning. Now a retired teacher, he has found enjoyable work as a volunteer at his town's home for the elderly. His former students call occasionally, and for a few he has become a figure of inspiration and wisdom—although Ernie would dispute both of those terms. Active in civic life and a patron of the local library and theater, he is nonetheless nearly invisible to most people. But for those few who have come to know him well, Ernie is both attractive and a bit unsettling. To describe fully how he came to be so would require more than a novel, but we can sketch the developmental stages he has traversed by looking at the study of ego development.

Ego Development: Making Sense of Life's Different Parts

Jane Loevinger (b. 1918), who is the key early researcher in the field, laid out her discoveries in her 1976 book *Ego Development*.[1] Spurred by her own experience of being discriminated against as a woman in the field of psychology, she began studying the lives and roles of women. Out of this research, and with its later expansion to men's lives as well, came a theory of stages and transitions in how we balance, organize, and make sense out of our lives as a whole——in short, how the ego, the organizing center of the personality, matures. For completeness' sake, we can look very briefly at the childhood stages, and then go quickly on to the typical adult stages and then to the stages of adult development that are beyond the present attainment of most adults. And since ego development serves in a way as the orchestra conductor of development, we can point out aspects of cognitive, moral, faith, and psychosexual development along the way. Table 4 can serve as a simplified guide to her discoveries.[2]

Table 4. Stages of Ego Development

Stage	Some characteristics of the stage:
Presocial	No awareness of self
Symbiotic	Separation of self from objects, not yet from mother
Impulsive	Attention to bodily impulses
Self-protective	Fear of discovery for wrongdoing; blame placed on others
Conformist	Fitting in to others' expectations; following accepted patterns
Conscientious-conformist (or Self-aware)	Beginnings of self-awareness as an individual with distinctive desires, preferences, wants, etc.
Conscientious	Self-chosen standards and values; ability to deal with complexity

Continued next page

Table 4 continued

Individualistic	Discovery of effects of self's & others' histories, social settings, etc.
Autonomous	Increased ability to manage conflicting inner values and desires peaceably
Integrated	Reconciliation of inner conflicts in paradox

Ego Development: The Early Stages

Ernie did not have an ego before or just after his birth; he was, as every infant is, completely submerged (we might say embedded) in the world of sensation. Loevinger would call this the time of the *presocial stage* (before Piaget's object constancy has been discovered), and the *symbiotic stage* (after object constancy, but while the infant still has no sense of a self differentiated from the mother).[3] Because the infant (from the Latin literally "without speech") does not yet have use of language, none of us can later "tell the story" of our own lives at this time; whatever memories were formed were not coded into language, and exist only as feelings or images that may arise from time to time. We might recall Fowler's emphasis on the continuing importance of such feelings in his description of the infant's early undifferentiated faith in chapter 5, and the vital role of touch and holding in the phase of sexual unawareness in chapter 6. The very young person does not have a conscious sense of self separate from her perceptions, nor the ability to form concepts about her experience. This embeddedness in perception means that very early experience engraves itself on us through feelings and moods which, although not stored in memory as concepts or words, nonetheless will be part of the foundation for our later lives.

Ernie, like most infants, joined his innate impulses to his growing abilities with words in the next, *impulsive* stage. Here his favorite word was "No!" His desire to do things for himself regularly conflicted with the well-meaning and often necessary interventions of his parents, and his budding sense of morality was engaged: the people around him could cause him pleasure, or pain (recall Kohlberg's preconventional stage one moral reasoning, in which morality is judged on just such terms). This budding sense of morality will influence development into the next ego-stage, called the *self-protective*. Now Ernie could anticipate short-term consequences, and learn to control his impulses according to what he could foresee as consequences. We might note resonances here with the phases of sexual awakening and later sexual surreptitiousness. Ernie could anticipate pleasure from his explorations; and he could also learn, as parents and society inevitably showed discomfort with his budding adventurousness, that he had best avoid potential punishment by hiding some of his discoveries from others. Thus Ernie moved through later childhood and into his adolescence.

Ego Development: Adulthood and Beyond

Loevinger's next stage is what she calls *conformist*; in it, Ernie discovered that he was a member of a group, and was expected to play a certain role in the group. He also found that he drew satisfaction from performing well in his assigned role. Here we can recall the importance of role taking in Kohlberg's stage three with its emphasis on interpersonal relationships as the foundation for moral decisions; in Fowler's synthetic-conventional (level three) faith; and even in all three levels of

Cavanagh's stage two, adolescent sexuality, with its emphasis on meeting one's own needs through interaction with others. When we remember that these developmental levels across all the areas of morality, sexuality, and faith are not rare in adults, we should not be surprised that Loevinger finds this stage of ego development common in adults as well. The orchestra and its conductor develop apace.

But Ernie had hardly conformed in the Vietnam era. He had decided and acted from a postconventional level of moral development, one that based choices on values that were more fundamental than society's customs or even its laws. And so it would not be surprising to find that Ernie was, even in his late teens, also beyond the conformist ego stage. The transition out of conformity to the group is based on the discovery of one's individuality, and with that the consequent awareness that as an individual it is possible to make choices other than those which seem within the group proper and perhaps even inevitable. These two developments—self-awareness and awareness of multiple possibilities—mark the onset of the *conscientious-conformist* or *self-aware* level. (Loevinger called it a "level" not a stage because the research did not make it clear whether it is a stage or a time of transition between stages.)[4] It, too, is common in adults in contemporary society, as a glance around us should show. Interest in one's own psychological makeup, when it is genuine and not simply the following of a cultural fad, is a marker of just this sort of growing awareness of one's distinctiveness and one's difference from others.

We can also note here that the "individualism" in American culture that is so often condemned by some pundits may well be a positive development for the persons so described and, as we will see in a moment, for society as well. People whose focus is on the self more than on their role in society may indeed be selfish, but they also may not be. It is equally possible that they are growing beyond the conformist level. Which of these is happening in any particular individual is difficult to tell from the outside. And since no one can understand a developmental level she or he has not yet attained, we should not be surprised that the self-aware level is misunderstood, mischaracterized, and condemned by people for whom, if they are still embedded in the conformist level, it is incomprehensible and thus a threat. This was Ernie's fate at the time he fled to Canada. Transition to the self-aware level can always be expected to come at the price of some degree of conflict, both internal and external. But it is hardly the last step in development. The "individualism" so often condemned by some may well be a positive development for the person and for society as well.

Beyond Conformity: An Individual Self

Self-awareness creates the possibility of individual conscience. Before we are quite aware of ourselves as individuals, our moral choices are inevitably mixed in with the attitudes (and often prejudices) of our group. So the next stage of ego development, after one has passed through the transition of the self-aware level, is the *conscientious stage*.[5] We may imagine the difference between the two this way: Ernie's departure for Canada may well have had a touch of the romantic rebel about it. While arguing with his father he would fall back on slogans because, although he was developing a firm sense of his values, he did not yet hold those values objectively enough to understand them and to explain them. Again, when we are embedded in a value we are "had by it" in Kegan's phrase.[6] We do not have the value, it "has us." Another transformation, the attainment of another stage with its enlarged perspective, will be required if we are to be able to see clearly what it is we value and so truly "have it." Before that our values are too close to us to come into clear focus, however firmly we may be guided by them.

His exile from his family and culture forced Ernie to come to terms with who he was as an individual, and with what he valued. He had to explain himself to himself. While doing this work on himself he learned what he would truly take to heart as his values, his ideals, and his goals. He learned to be self-critical and responsible for his choices not because his role required it but because his choices, ideals, and values were now clearly and in a new way his own. And because he could now see himself clearly as distinct from other people, he could also for the first time see other people clearly as similarly unique and valuable. So through his own growth he became newly responsible to others and for their well-being. At the conscientious stage any self-preoccupation that may accompany self-awareness is largely left behind. So pundits might rest easier if they could become aware that the solution to the "problem of individualism" is not to scold people into returning to conformism (which, because of the one-way nature of development, is impossible in any case), but to encourage them to move more deeply into self-awareness. Of course, if critics and commentators are themselves embedded in the conformist stage, they will be unable to understand this and may well find the idea threatening—first to themselves. If people continue to grow, care for others will re-emerge in a new and deeper form in the conscientious stage.

Ernie's choice to become a teacher is not surprising. But why he chose the role and how he fulfilled his responsibilities in it would differ from those who might take a teaching job because of external benefits or out of respect for family or cultural forces. For Ernie his teaching was a vocation, not a job or a role. He would measure his achievements by his own standards, perhaps seeming a bit odd to school administrators. And he would have an inner life more complex than many of his peers. His developing interest in the arts fed and expressed this complexity. And by this interest he was laying the groundwork for yet more growth.

Individuality and Awareness of One's History

Over time Ernie's growing awareness of his own complexity and others' led him to a sense of his life as embedded in a history and in a web of emotional dependencies. By noticing this he was, of course, stepping out of his embeddedness in that web. Until now he had always been a product of his history and woven into these dependencies; he was simply unable to see it. But by gaining perspective on the unique history of himself and, by extension, of each person in his life, Ernie grew beyond even the conscientious stage. This deepening appreciation for one's unique history and setting marks a transition (through what Loevinger calls the *individualistic level*) to the next, *autonomous stage*.[7]

Difficulties in Understanding the Later Stages of Development

It would not be surprising to feel a bit of dizziness at this point. For one thing, as ego development progresses the person's unique individuality comes more and more to the fore; hence it becomes harder to describe, except in very abstract terms. For another, we are now quite possibly passing beyond the developmental level at which each of us is embedded, and so even the best description would leave us puzzled. And finally, it may well be that even the researchers studying these levels are not yet sufficiently developed to understand them from their own experience, as Loevinger notes.[8] And so they have something of a tin ear as they try to describe the music of these advanced stages, and they leave us with only the words. Loevinger would describe Ernie at the autonomous stage as able to cope with conflicts arising from his complex inner experience, as having a vivid sense of his emotional life and his feelings, and as respecting both people's autonomy and their interdependence. He would habitually see himself, others, and relationships in their wider social and historical setting.

And just as Cavanagh supplies in his final phase of adult sexuality, psychosexual integration,[9] a way to appreciate that adult development is open-ended, so Loevinger suggests a stage beyond autonomy, which she calls the *integrated* stage of ego development.[10] This would involve Ernie's growing peace with what he had experienced at the autonomous stage as conflicting pressures, his sense of connection to what is ultimately real, and a sense of participation in a oneness that transcends all divisions.

While it is doubtful that Ernie has reached this final stage, the fact that some former students continue to look to him as a figure of wisdom and inspiration suggests that his ego level does exert a sort of gravitational pull on those who desire to grow. This is typical of development's more advanced stages. Transformation is often helped by the presence of someone one stage ahead of one's present level. Ernie's postconventional perspective will be a puzzle to many, and perhaps a threat. But for a few, he represents their own next step.

Having looked at various strands of development through the lifespan, we can turn to the question: What do they say about each person's life journey as a whole? It is time to step back and to see how the pieces fit together.

Questions for Reflection and Discussion

1. Whom have you ever met who seemed to you to be an exceptionally peaceful and integrated person? What was your reaction to him or to her? How can you connect what you discovered there to the material presented in this chapter?

2. How do you react to the chapter's approach to the "individualism" so often criticized today? What are the differences between morally objectionable selfishness and the search for individuality described here? Why might they be confused by observers and social critics?

3. What feelings emerge as you think about the levels of development that are still beyond you? Is the prospect of further change attractive, or threatening, or both?

EIGHT

✑

Taking Stock

We have met toddlers and seniors, Amanda and her grandmother Pauline. Among their friends have been struggling adults like George, and people like his older brother Ernie who seem to have made something quietly remarkable of their lives. Along the way we touched on how we learn to reason through Piaget's work; with Kohlberg on our ways of making moral decisions; through Fowler, on the development of mature faith; on psychosexual development with Cavanagh; and finally on the unifying ego in the work of Loevinger. Is there a single overview that would help us to make sense of our explorations?

Unfortunately, no. Human beings are too complex to allow any one theory to explain us simply and comprehensively. But keeping that and a few additional warnings in mind, we can draw the threads together. We begin with the cautions.

Thinking Carefully about Development

First, we should remember that all psychological research and theory making is more like a flashlight than a set of pigeonholes. These discoveries may, if used well, illuminate for our awareness things we see in ourselves and others but may not have understood. Developmental theories that speak of levels or stages, as these have, mean to draw our attention to relatively fixed patterns of thought and action that persist in individuals for months or years or decades, and to the predictable transitions and order by which we shift from one such stable pattern to another. In all the areas we have looked at, such stages and transitions occur. And they occur within each area of our lives in a fixed order, without skipping steps or moving permanently backward. No one, for example, who has reached the adult phase called psychosexual mutuality can be expected to return to a consistent pattern of adolescent sexual fantasy (except perhaps in cases of psychosis or brain damage). No teenager reaching formal operational thinking will revert to the preoperational level. No one of individuative-reflective faith will step back to mythic-literal faith.

Similarly, no one seems to be able to skip over levels. Moral thinking moves only through stage two fairness on the way to stage three role playing and approval of others, never around it. And the transitions between stages are in each case what we have called type two change or transformation, not simply the addition of new facts to one's existing knowledge. Recall how Haughton described the flow of transformation: It contains first remote preparation (both within and around the person, the existing stage and also a culture that holds out an invitation to something more); then the creation of a weak spot; third, the inexplicable shift itself; and finally a period of consolidation in the new perspective. You may recall that we used falling in love and getting the point of a riddle as examples.

A Rough Guide:
Preconventional, Conventional,
and Postconventional Levels

We also saw that it is not unusual for adults to live for years or decades—perhaps even the rest of life—in a stage before the final one. Kohlberg calls his levels three and four "conventional";[1] Loevinger remarks that the transition between her stages three and four is a stable outlook for many adults.[2] And Fowler calls his stage three faith "synthetic-conventional."[3] Thus along most of the strands of development we could, even if all the researchers do not, group levels into three wide categories: those typically experienced before one is an adult in this culture; those typical for many adults; and those only occasionally seen when some adults develop beyond what is typical. We could borrow Kohlberg's terminology, which some others have also extended in this way, and describe these three wide levels as preconventional, conventional, and postconventional.[4] Thus we might say that for Piaget the sensorimotor, preoperational, and concrete operational stages are preconventional; and that formal operations is the conventional stage of development for adults as we usually meet them. (Piaget's research focused mostly on children and adolescents, and did not address whether there are postconventional stages of understanding to be discovered.)

For Kohlberg we have seen the preconventional level with its stages of pleasure/punishment and of fairness; the conventional level of mutual interpersonal relationships and later of reliance on social systems and law; and the postconventional level attained by some, beginning in the "prior-to-society" perspective and developing finally into awareness of and commitment to universal ethical principles. With regard to faith, we could judge Fowler's stages zero (undifferentiated), one (intuitive-projective), and two (mythic-literal) faith preconventional; his stage three (synthetic-conventional) we might concur and call conventional; and consider his stages four (individuative-reflective), five (conjunctive), and six (universalizing) faith as postconventional.

Loevinger's description of ego development names the level three-four (or self-aware) transition (between the conformist and conscientious stages) as frequently found in adults; so we could well consider this range as the typical or conventional level for ego development, and call preconventional her presocial, symbiotic, impulsive, and self-protective stages; and postconventional the conscientious, individualistic, autonomous, and integrated stages.

With regard to psychosexual development such a breakdown is harder, although we could at least say that childhood sexuality (sexual unawareness, awakening, and surreptitiousness) and at least the first two phases of adolescent sexuality (fantasy and preoccupation) are typically grown through and passed beyond by many adults. It would be harder to say whether adolescent phase three (superficial sexual relating) has frequently been left behind, although certainly many have arrived at adult phase one, psychosexual mutuality. And psychosexual integration may well be considered postconventional.

So far the strands have been considered separately; but dividing them into preconventional, conventional, and postconventional levels invites us to lay them side by side, as Table 5 shows (next page).

And now we can ask, are there relationships "across the rows," so that there is some necessary or natural linkage among, say, formal operations, synthetic-conventional faith, and a conformist ego-level?

Although it appears to make sense, that research has yet to be done. In a few cases it seems likely. (Fowler, for instance, makes connections between Piaget's concrete operational

Table 5. Stages of Development Compared

	Piaget: cognition	Kohlberg: moral	Fowler: faith	Cavanagh: psychosexual	Loevinger: ego
Preconventional	Sensorimotor Preoperational Concrete operations	Punishment Fairness	Undifferentiated Intuitive-projective Mythic-literal	Unawareness Awakening Surreptitiousness Fantasy Preoccupation	Presocial Symbiotic Impulsive Self-protective
Conventional	Formal operations	Reciprocal roles Societal rules	Synthetic-conventional	Superficial sexual relating Mutuality	Conformist Self-aware
Postconventional	(Not addressed)	Prior-to-society Universal principles	Individuative-reflective Conjunctive Universalizing	Integration	Conscientious Individualistic Autonomous Integrated

thinking and his mythic-literal faith, and links formal operations with synthetic-conventional faith.)[5] There may be other such dependencies. And although it would go beyond the evidence at this point to make further connections of specific stages, we may be on firmer ground at least to suspect that we can generalize about the transition from preconventional to conventional to postconventional levels or stages in the different aspects of life.

Growing into the Conventional Stages of Development

The image of embeddedness is the place to start. Recall that Kegan uses this to describe how, at every point in our lives, some attitudes, concepts, values, and understandings are so intimately bound up with who we are that we cannot find a point of view outside them to see them for what they are; they are too much a part of us. We do not, as he says, have them; they have us embedded within them. (Patriotism of the "my country right or wrong" variety would be an example of a value that so possesses a person that she is embedded in it.) Development is marked by transformations in understanding; we learn to step out from what we had been embedded in so that we can see it and appreciate it and evaluate it. We then can decide, if we wish, to remain related to that attitude or value or understanding by choosing to embrace it; but we are free with regard to it. We have a place to stand outside it. But of course this place to stand is itself embedded in a new and more complex (and, it is to be hoped, more accurate) perspective on ourselves, other people, and the world.

Every society faces the challenge of making each new generation into effective members. It wants them, we might say, to become embedded in the ways of looking at things and in the values that constitute that society. Nothing is so powerful as that which comes to be taken for granted as "just the way things are." So society has a reason to invest time and energy and resources in helping people to develop from preconventional to conventional levels of understanding (which is why schools assist children to coming to formal operational thinking); of moral judgment (for which we have moral and legal codes as well as informal rewards and punishments for "fitting in" or not); of psychosexual development (which is nurtured through the formal institution of marriage as well as by countless informal expectations presented by families and peer groups). And religious institutions similarly hope and try to bring their members by the time they are adults from undifferentiated faith through the preconventional stages to synthetic-conventional faith.

In short, the growing child and teenager will come upon countless opportunities to step out of embeddedness in preconventional perspectives. The society provides Haughton's climate of remote preparation, and also her weak spots. And because of their number and diversity these can generally be trusted. They will lead most young people to the breakthroughs that will lift them out of embeddedness at preconventional stages. And then youngsters will find that society offers supports for the consolidation of these breakthroughs: There will be rewards and affirmation, from increased freedom to financial opportunities to the praise of others, that will stabilize them in society's conventional outlook. That embeddedness in conventional perspectives is common should be no surprise; society has made a significant investment in helping each member to grow to that, and is itself created and sustained in each generation by the efforts of those successfully socialized people, as we saw with George and Martha and Michelle and Tim.

Resistance to Postconventional Stages

When it comes to postconventional levels the story is different. The transformation beyond conventional stages requires breaking out of embeddedness in what society takes for granted. (As the adage goes, "It's a wise fish that knows it lives in water.") Disembedding may occasionally result in dramatic conflict (as with Ernie and with other political dissenters through the ages). Or it may be quieter and less public, but still uncomfortable for all those touched by it. (The person of devout synthetic-conventional faith who is struggling to disembed herself from it may feel as if, and be told by worried religious leaders that, she is "losing her faith.") There are few societal institutions to support this disembedding, and many to resist it. The individual may have to search out examples to imitate (among her peers or in history), rather than having them thrust at her. Movement to more advanced levels may not be praised and rewarded but instead be questioned and sanctioned, because an objective perspective on what society assumes unquestioningly is disturbing to any society. Even if such a perspective is not expressed in overt disobedience to customs or laws, a stance that makes it clear that one's adoption of a society's assumptions is a *choice* and *not* an *inevitability* can disrupt social peace; and so it is always widely suspect.

Because of all this it should not be surprising that adult development seems to pause or stop for many people in the conventional stages.[6] Development is hard, and sometimes risky. It is more surprising that not a few people do continue to grow. How they do so would no doubt retell the story of the four-stage transformation process: seek out a supportive climate; look for, or engineer a weak spot; surrender (perhaps with considerable fear) to letting go of what has been taken for granted; and then commit to maintaining the new perspective through the hard work of finding resources that help one to consolidate it.[7] This process can shed light on the role of spirituality in development, which is the subject of our next chapter.

Questions for Reflection and Discussion

1. What sorts of rewards exist in today's culture for "fitting in"? How is disapproval for not fitting in expressed? How does society punish those who don't or can't fit in?
2. When someone doesn't share society's conventional perspectives, how can you tell whether that person has not yet grown to adopt them, or has grown beyond them? That is, how do you tell preconventional from postconventional perspectives? What can make it difficult or impossible to tell them apart?
3. What benefits come to a society from allowing the expression of postconventional ideas? What are the costs of allowing it?

NINE

Spiritual Practice

Let us take leave of our imaginary family and their friends, and turn in this chapter to our own experience. Begin by recalling two familiar Gospel stories, often called "tribute to Caesar" and "the woman caught in adultery." In both, Jesus is seemingly entrapped by his adversaries. "Tribute to Caesar" (Mark 12:13–17 and parallels) is about whether to pay taxes to the hated Roman occupying force. If Jesus forbids payment, he risks from the Romans a charge of subversion; if he allows it, from his Jewish neighbors one of collaboration with the enemy. "The woman caught in adultery" (John 8:3–11) invites Jesus to set himself against either the Law of Moses (if he objects to the woman's punishment), or against his own teaching of a merciful God and against the Roman law forbidding such punishments (if he agrees).

Spiritual Mastery: Accurate Perception and Appropriate Action

You already know how each story ends. But note exactly how remarkable Jesus' response is in both cases. If we were unfamiliar with the Gospels, it would be almost inconceivable that we could on our own come up with something to say in each case that was so exactly appropriate to all the conflicting forces. And yet as we look back on what Jesus did say, it seems so simple and obviously right. "Give to the emperor the things that are the emperor's, and to God the things that are God's" (Mark 12:17). "Let anyone among you who is without sin be the first to throw a stone at her" (John 8:7). The replies fit like the right key to a lock. They seem to be at the same time utterly ordinary and down to earth, and also to bring a new perspective that is self-evidently right but until that point unimaginable.

If you think otherwise, that Jesus' replies are inventive but not extraordinary, try two experiments. First, see how many other examples of such accuracy and appropriateness you can find, in literature and in the media; and more tellingly, call to mind how often you have been in a bind and said something that did not quite hit the mark, even if it was not the perfectly wrong thing to say. There are a few examples of elegant accuracy matching Jesus' in the world's spiritual literature, especially in teaching stories of the great rabbis, Zen-masters, and the like. But in these stories too we find remarks that are both utterly right and seemingly ordinary once we have heard them, and also clearly beyond our ability to come up with on our own. Understanding this is a path to understanding what spirituality is about. Spiritual masters see the ordinary world we live in much more accurately than we do, and so they can act within it more appropriately.

The Role of Practice

People often misunderstand spirituality as something otherworldly. For a Christian, nothing could be more wrong. We believe that God created the world; that God cares for and sustains the world; and that God so loved the world as to become human within it: "The Word became flesh and lived among us" (John 1:14). And our ultimate hope is not to be rescued from the world, but to live forever in a world transformed fully by God's loving care. We might learn more of what spirituality is truly for if we revived an ancient phrase and talked not about spirituality but instead about *spiritual practice.*

We know what practice involves. We do it with our golf swing, at the piano, in public-speaking classes. Parents spend hours driving children to practice for soccer, for ballet, for their SATs. Practice is the way we master a skill, get better at doing something—improve our accuracy at fitting our performance to the requirements of the situation. If the lie of the golf ball requires that we loft the ball over an obstacle and then stop it quickly when it hits the green, we may know that but not be able to do it unless we have practiced doing so. Practice leads to assessing the situation expertly and being able to do what needs to be done in that situation. Spiritual practice is no different, and this is where it connects to development.

> *Practice is the way we master a skill, get better at doing something. We improve our accuracy at fitting our performance to the requirements of the situation.*

Practice and Development

Think of an infant's experience before she has discovered what Piaget called object permanence.[1] She will consistently make mistakes—assessing her situation wrongly and so responding to it inaccurately. (Piaget's research shows how consistently and predictably inaccurate she will be, the consistency coming exactly from her misunderstanding of what the world is like.) Her constant interaction with a world that surprises her by being different from what she expects will teach her, in time, to improve her assessment of how objects behave—she will learn that they remain in existence even when out of sight. Although at this age she does not "practice" in a conventional sense, every moment is in its way a set of experiments which teach her when her perspective is correct (and makes good predictions) and when it is not (making bad ones). These "everyday experiments" are her practice, and that practice leads to her development.

Or take an adult example. Experienced nurses in neonatal intensive care units have been shown to be able consistently to detect when premature infants are coming down with severe infections even before clinical tests indicate anything wrong.[2] Their training and experience have led them to perceive such infants' condition with an accuracy that is demonstrable, even though they commonly cannot describe what it is that they have learned to notice. Inexperienced nurses cannot see the warning signs so soon. While not a stage change in the sense we have been exploring, we see again how development is marked by more accurate perception and more effective response. Experienced nurses see the infants' danger before others do, and so can act to protect them. A more-developed "stage" (of nursing skill or of golfing ability or of ego development) allows one to assess some part of experience more accurately and to respond more appropriately than a person who has not developed to such a level can.

Practice, Development, and Accurate Perception

Take another adult example, this time one which does involve stages of personality development. Recall the description in chapter 5 of Tim's unease with his son Eddie's religious drawings. Tim was uncomfortable because his stage four individuative-reflective faith was, for all its rational development, unable to find a place for the symbolic and transrational dimensions on which Eddie's drawings touched in their own childish way. We might say now that Tim must leave stage four faith behind if he is to appreciate the world more accurately, making space for both the rational and the poetic dimensions of life. Without the poetry of symbols, life is simply not perceived accurately enough. Stage change is growth toward more accurate perception, and with that clearer perception comes the possibility of more appropriate action.

"Higher" stages of development—cognitive, moral, faith, psychosexual, and ego—do not make more accurate perception and more appropriate action inevitable; no one is exempt from laziness, selfishness, and of course sin. But just as a marksman stands a better chance of hitting her target with a properly-adjusted gun sight and a well-made rifle than with poorer tools, later stages of development make accurate perception and fitting action more predictably possible and less a matter of lucky chance.

Later stages of development make accurate perception and fitting action more predictably possible and less a matter of lucky chance.

Development, Holiness, and Skill

Still, it would be a mistake to confuse *development* with *holiness*. Holiness is a matter of what we do with the gifts we have at any moment, and those gifts include our present level of development. A child or a teenager or an adult at any stage can be holy; he can do the best it is possible for him to do at that moment. But there will be new possibilities for a different sort of holiness when he has developed further. He may not grasp these possibilities, due to laziness or sin; but the new possibilities will not even exist without development. For example: The grace of sacramental marriage, faithful and life-long, is not a possibility to an adolescent (in development, not age); he or she will have to grow into an adult stage of psychosexual development either before the ceremony or after, if the holiness that is possible to a marriage partner is to become a possibility. As the Catholic tradition insists, grace builds on nature. And part of our nature at every moment is our developmental level.

If we think again about Jesus' comments we see that they are *exactly* appropriate to all the dimensions of his situation. He assessed the scene more clearly than we can, and he responded more appropriately. Simply put, he was *freer* than we are. When we look back at what he said, the accuracy of his assessment and the appropriateness of his response are made clear by how perfectly and simply his responses fit. This is the goal of every practice: *to be able to act consistently in a fitting way*. Spiritual practice has the same goal, to help us to learn to perceive accurately all the dimensions of the visible and invisible world as God gives it to us; and so to learn how to act appropriately in God's world—to become more free. Psychological development is not the goal of spiritual practice, but may well accompany it. To see why, we can examine some of the components that most spiritual practices share.

The goal of spiritual practice is to help us learn to perceive accurately all the dimensions of the visible and invisible world as God gives it to us; and so to learn how to act appropriately in God's world—to become more free.

Spiritual Practices That Invite Development

The first component is *reflection*. Spiritual practice involves stopping our active lives regularly to consider the outcomes of our actions. If we are consistent, we may come to discover that sometimes things turn out badly because we have not properly understood what was required of us. (It may be illuminating to notice how many times in the Gospels Jesus upbraids his disciples not for lack of effort but because they do not, in his word, "see." That is, they do not understand the world from the proper perspective.) If we learn to suspect that we too do not now see things aright, we may cast about for help (from God and/or others), and may become ready to learn from those who seem more consistently to perceive things more accurately than we do.

The second component of spiritual practice is *asceticism*; we might better call it *self-discipline*. From fasting to celibacy, self-discipline is a tactic to establish a consistent and balanced relationship between our instinctive energies and our guiding ego. Self-discipline is not to suppress the instincts but to channel them and make them ready to hand when their energy is needed in pursuit of chosen goals. Development similarly aims, ultimately, at unification or at least coordination of the diverse parts of ourselves. It is no accident that the final, open-ended stages of ego- and psychosexual development are called *integrated*.

The third component is *guidance*. This can come personally from a spiritual director or guru, or from the wisdom of a tradition. Anyone who has once taken a tennis lesson understands that what feels "natural" to a beginner needs correction. And what at first feels like an awkward way of doing things will, over time as a skill is mastered, reveal itself as the economical and graceful way. Guidance saves us the work of re-learning for ourselves the wisdom of accumulated experience. We have already seen that the presence and example of someone functioning at a higher stage of development is often the challenge and guide to one's own progressive transformation.

The fourth component of spiritual practice is *a symbolic life*. Expressed in art, ritual, and commonly both, spiritual practice relies on modes of communication and awareness that encompass and transcend the rational. Symbols have the remarkable power to speak a different language to people at different levels of development. Little Eddie can draw his pictures of Moses or Jesus and be enraptured by the (pre-rational) images. Adult Tim needs art and ritual and poetry to draw him beyond the once-liberating but now also confining prose of rationality. Exactly because we cannot fully comprehend them, symbols (whether they be objects or actions) draw us into a wider world than we know, preparing the ground and creating the weak spot Haughton describes as a precondition for further transformation.[3]

The fifth component is *gratitude for gifts*. Spiritual practice invites us to recognize all of our experience as not simply dumb facts, but as invitations to a meeting. Gifts imply a Giver; gifts are implicit promises, holding out the hope that what is given is not the last word but that the Giver offers himself. Here there are two prompts to development. First, a world of givers and receivers of gifts—of *exchange*[4] in Rosemary Haughton's wonderful image—is more complex and more intriguing than a world of brute facts; it helps us to suspect a wider world than we now experience. Second, an awareness that all we experience is a gift invites us to a sense of humility in the face of existence. It is easier to understand that our grasp of the world is partial and provisional if we are clear that we are not self-sufficient.

An Example from Liturgical Practice

It may help our understanding to recall a lesson taught by the Catholic Church to those preparing for adult baptism. Three weeks before Easter, at the second of the Scrutinies (times of public prayer for those to be initiated), the Gospel passage of the "man born blind" is read (John 9). The Gospel and the ritual invite the Elect and the congregation to a transformation from blindness to seeing. Using sight as a metaphor for understanding, the wisdom of the ritual points out the goal of all spiritual practice: to understand more accurately, and so be able to act more appropriately. And what is to be understood is not some esoteric knowledge, but simply the way the world—God's world—*is*. Spiritual practice for the Christian is meant to make us more effective disciples, but not by taking us away from ordinary living. The point of practice is to become a more effective disciple by becoming a more effective human being, one who comprehends more accurately each situation in which she discovers herself. Through practice she comes to "see" in a way that she formerly did not. Again, development does not guarantee holiness; greater understanding can, when distorted by selfishness and fear and the other vices, make for more effective application of one's energies to evil ends. But while someone at any level of development may be holy, in the sense of doing the best with the understanding he has at any moment, limited development almost guarantees limited effectiveness despite the person's best efforts.

> *The point of spiritual practice is to become a more effective disciple by becoming a more effective human being, one who comprehends more accurately each situation in which she discovers herself.*

Spiritual practice and developmental awareness intersect neatly with the Bible phrase that has been our theme: *We are God's children now.* Fear stymies change. No one takes a step if it appears to be into an abyss. Development takes courage, nourished from successes in meeting the challenges of each developmental stage. The reassurance that we are God's children provides a foundation for taking the risk to step into the unknown future when the possibility offers itself. Transformation is always a step out of comfortable embeddedness in one's present world. *What we will be has not yet been brought to light.* No future stage is imaginable from the perspective of the previous one. Like seeing the joke in a pub riddle, the next stage will be obvious after we have taken the step, but obscure before. God has a dream for what we shall be; we cannot yet understand it, but we grow toward it as we develop. *What we do know is this: when he is revealed, we will be like him, for we will see him as he is.* The goal of development, as of spiritual practice, is ultimately simple (although hard to describe and harder to attain). It is, adapting the words of the thirteenth-century English bishop Richard of Chichester, to "know…more clearly, love…more dearly, and follow [Christ] more nearly, day by day."[5]

Developmental thinking can also help us in understanding aspects of church ministry and mission, especially by making clear some reasons that people are engaged or not engaged by various church activities. The next chapter explores an example. *Stewardship* is a relatively new term and topic in Catholic circles, and our appreciation of stages of development may help us to understand how people hear the invitation to become stewards—and why they sometimes cannot.

Questions for Reflection and Discussion

1. What were you taught about the purpose of spiritual practices? How does the perspective presented here fit with that teaching? How does it alter the meaning of spiritual practice from what you were taught?
2. Beyond the examples of Jesus here, what other examples of spiritual masters' accuracy of perception can you think of?
3. Can you think of examples of how more accurate perception can also make it possible for a person to be more effective in doing evil? What does a person need beyond development in order to be effective at doing good?

TEN

∽

Developmental Thinking: A Practical Application

Sometimes it helps to imagine that people at different developmental levels live in different worlds. This chapter applies such developmental thinking to a practical issue in church life, stewardship and especially sacrificial giving. Since the publication in 1993 of the U.S. Catholic Bishops' pastoral letter *Stewardship: A Disciple's Response*,[1] many Catholic parishes have attempted to put into place programs to encourage giving based on stewardship principles. But education about stewardship has not often taken into account the hearers of the message. Because Catholic adults (like adults in every religious denomination and every culture) are at different developmental levels, it may be necessary to enter a variety of "worlds" to speak effectively to all. And since we commonly assume that people are, deep down, "just like us," it may be no surprise that the stewardship message is often crafted in the language that makes sense to the speaker but not to the hearer. As you read this chapter you will be invited to use your own awareness of developmental levels to translate the stewardship message. If the goal of communication is to get a message across successfully, we are wiser to do the translation ourselves rather than to rely on our hearers, who

108

may not have the privilege of developmental awareness, to do the translation for themselves.

People's motives for giving have been widely studied by scholars, fund-raisers, and church leaders.[2] Most agree that people who give expect to receive something back for their gift. But what sorts of things do people hope to receive? A glance at the different appeals that arrive regularly in the mailbox or from the pulpit will show that people are promised everything from material prosperity to eternal life, from answered prayers to feelings of self-satisfaction for their generosity. Being by now trained detectives, we can look at this diversity and draw a conclusion: Fund-raisers have discovered that people are diverse, and that different people respond positively to different sorts of appeals. But we can now bring our own developmental perspective to the questions: What motivates people to give? And why do some appeals leave us cold?

Think of a few examples. You may be repelled by promises that giving to a television preacher will make you rich, but some people do send money. You may find the public acknowledgement of major donors sensible, or you may think that anonymity is better. Each of us has a sense of what motives for giving make sense, and we find that people who seem to be motivated in other ways leave us puzzled. Again we have unsettled our assumption that, at least deep down, people are just like we are. Now we know that this perspective is limited; people at different developmental stages see aspects of the world differently, and so people at stages different from our own are *not* like us.

But people who design fund-raising appeals can fall into this trap of presumed similarity, and so may ask others to give only for reasons that they themselves find sensible. An awareness of the stages of adult development can bring two advantages: (1) We can understand why certain sorts of appeal may resonate with people at certain stages of growth, and (2) we can remember to address people in ways that may not be natural to us, but that speak to them in ways they can understand while still respecting our values and our ultimate goals.

Developmental Differences in How a Message Is Heard

If we look back at early stages of development—notably Kohlberg's stage two fairness and its equivalent in Loevinger's self-protective stage two, we might appreciate that some people in our congregations are not able to understand appeals framed in lofty concepts—not because they do not understand the *words*, but because the words appeal to *motives* they cannot comprehend. Their world is one in which the primary motive is (short-term) fair exchange. They want to experience something that seems to be a just trade in their giving, what we might call quid-pro-quo or "tit-for-tat." It might make sense to them to give only if they can expect to see their name on a plaque in the church. Not to offer some tangible reward would make giving seem like an unfair exchange. Or they might gladly volunteer their time, but feel slighted were there to be no public acknowledgement of their efforts.

We might regard people at such a level of motivation for giving as being at *"stage one: give-to-get (tangible)."* That is, giving makes sense only when it exists within a context of fair exchange and the reward for giving is something that can be seen and touched—a memorialized statue, or a plaque, or a luncheon, or the like. A stewardship message that ignores fair and tangible exchange will be incoherent to such people. It may seem awkward to others (including perhaps the program's sponsors and leaders) who have developed beyond this stage, but a successful leader makes it easy for her troops to follow; she does the translation, rather than insisting that they do it. So she translates the stewardship message into the language of "give to get" for those who live in that sort of world. The stewardship process, if it can learn to speak this language as well as other more complex ones, provides opportunities for more people to participate because they can understand the message. Otherwise, the stewardship appeal will sometimes be incomprehensible—or even threatening.

We know that emerging from embeddedness is a vital step in development. And it is common to observe that many churchgoers have in fact emerged from the tangible sort of "give-to-get" just described. They might say in comparison to their former stage that their motives are now "more spiritual," in that they do not seek a physical but rather an intangible reward for their giving. They might hope that their prayers will be heard and answered, or that someone they love will be spared suffering, or that their salvation will be made more likely, or that they will grow in God's grace through their gift. We might agree that this is a more developed sense of stewardship; but we might also note that it is still a sort of tit-for-tat, and might call it "*stage two: give to get (spiritual)*." It is not "better" in any moral sense than its predecessor; *any* giving may be a genuinely holy action if it is the best the person can do at the time given his present level of understanding. But from the outside we can see that stage two is a development beyond the stage one tangible give-to-get, and nearer to the stewardship ideal.

Beyond Short-Term Fairness

Exactly because human development progresses from tit-for-tat reciprocal relationships toward a level in which fulfilling a role within a family or community comes to take center stage (call to mind Loevinger's conformist stage and Kohlberg's stage three role dependency), it is not surprising that a new motive for giving emerges in parallel. When it becomes possible for an individual to grasp that it is expected that each member of a congregation will take some part in parish support, and that a mark of full participation in congregational life is the making of a regular and sacrificial offering, we see such a change in motive. Such a person has emerged from tit-for-tat, and might even be able to say that it is now no longer her reason to give. What the person is now embedded in is the role of a participant in the group; we might call it *"stage three: give to belong."* At this stage "everybody's doing it" becomes a motivator. If giving is presented as an expectation of the community to which one wants to belong, a person at this stage of development will understand the message and perhaps be moved to action by it.

So a stewardship appeal that wants to speak the language of people at stages one through three will have to ensure that it provides multiple paths to involvement: tangible memorials (for stage one), reason to hope for spiritual benefit (for stage two), and the affirmation that can be expected for meeting the legitimate expectations of one's community (for stage three). Each of these appeals may seem to diminish the altruism of the stewardship message; but what appears as appropriate altruism to a parish leader or committee is almost certainly influenced to some degree by their level of development. Again, one always tends to speak one's own "natural" language, and to be convinced that one's own perspective is the most legitimate one. Successful

communication between levels requires the effort of translation, so that the values of the message are not compromised
but the worldview of the intended hearer is respected as well.
It does no good to proclaim a "pure" message that is incomprehensible to its audience.

> *It does no good to proclaim a "pure" message that
> is incomprehensible to its audience.*

Motives Arising from Self-Awareness

So what might be the mental universe of the speaker who
creates a message that goes beyond what many hearers can
interpret? Here again it would not be surprising if further developmental levels play their part. Remember that Loevinger's
postconventional stages (beginning with the conscientious) are
marked by growing self-awareness and increasing responsibility
for one's self and values. Giving in this context can become a
means of furthering one's spiritual practice and an expression of
who one has become (one's values) and hopes to become (one's
aspirations). We might call the motive at this level "*stage four:
give to grow.*" The reference point has shifted away from what
one's companions are doing, and the point of reference has
returned to the self.

It might be interesting to note in passing here that this
postconventional level of development once again looks something like a preconventional one. How is the self-regard of
stage four give-to-grow different from stage two give-to-get?
The simplest and most profound difference is that stage two
has something of the nature of a contract and expectation,
even if what one hopes to receive is not clearly described.
Stage four in contrast has the nature of an experiment: What
will happen to me through disciplined sacrificial giving? How

will it change me? Not only does the difference between the stages become clear when posed this way, but it also becomes understandable that the motivation of someone at stage four is beyond the comprehension of someone at stage two, and may even appear threatening. On the other hand, when someone at stage three begins to find the possibility of such a step into the unknown to be intriguing, we see the beginnings of emergence and a step toward growth.

The Stewardship Message as an Invitation to Grow

This can be a reminder that the stewardship appeal cannot limit itself just to the languages and motives of stages one, two, and three. While it is important to speak the language of each developmental level sometimes, it is equally important to provide hints that there is more over the horizon of each level. People can in this way be challenged not only to give, but also to grow toward more full maturity in their motive for giving. And just as both Loevinger and Cavanagh include a final, open-ended level of development, we might do so too in looking at some of the saints and the sort of giving they seem to have practiced. If we ask, Did Saint Francis of Assisi or Blessed Mother Teresa of Calcutta "give to get"? That seems silly. "Give to belong"? No. "Give to grow"? Perhaps after a fashion, but from what we can understand about them even this sort of description seems not to do their motives adequate justice.

It may be better to hold out the possibility that giving can become such a part of someone's nature that the matter of motive seems almost to disappear. We might borrow a phrase from the mystic Meister Eckhart (ca. 1260–ca. 1329) and say that such rare individuals live at *"stage five: give 'without a why.'"*[3] A congregation full of such saints would hardly need stewardship appeals and reminders; and the fact that ours do need such care, and that we do as well, tells us that developmental levels have their influence even in such seemingly mundane aspects of life as parish support. And an awareness of the way we, and everyone around us, live in a mental world that is not shared universally but varies according to our level of development, can help us to understand, to appreciate, to communicate, and to serve—humbly, accurately, and effectively. We might summarize our thinking about giving as in Table 6.

Table 6. Motives for Giving

Stage & name	Motive for giving:
1: Give to get (tangible)	Fair exchange of gift for tangible reward
2: Give to get (spiritual)	Fair exchange of gift for spiritual reward
3: Give to belong	To feel a sense of belonging to the group
4: Give to grow	To experiment with how giving will change one
5: Give "without a why"	As part of who one has become, without motive

By thinking about stewardship and development together we can discover one instance that might help to answer the very practical question, What good does developmental awareness do? How can we be better off for having explored this way of thinking? But that issue deserves a chapter of its own.

Questions for
Reflection and Discussion

1. What sorts of appeals have you heard for contributions to charities? What developmental levels would you assign them to?
2. What feelings arise when you hear a message cast in a language that does not fit your own developmental level?
3. How might you use this awareness in your own family or neighborhood, or church or community group?

ELEVEN

❧

Putting What We Know to Work

Even though by this point you may feel that you have only a hazy understanding of the stages of human development (and it is true that there is far more to learn), you still know more about them than do most of the people you meet every day, indeed more than most human beings on this planet. And as Jesus said, "From everyone to whom much has been given, much will be required" (Luke 12:48); or in the more pithy maxim of the recovery movement, "When you know, you owe." So we have a responsibility to ourselves and to others not simply to put this book aside, but to try to make sense of what we can do even with our limited knowledge. There are three subsections in this chapter: How to avoid doing harm (to oneself or others); what one can do for oneself; and what one can offer to others. We begin with the warnings.

How to Avoid Doing Harm with This Information

First, do not claim to know more than you do about others. Nothing is more harmful to genuine dialogue than an assumption that we understand someone better than she does

117

herself. Do not try to explain to someone how he is embedded in a worldview that you can see objectively; even if this were true, you will not help things by making such a claim.

Second, do not use the language of stages and levels and transformation with anyone with whom you are in conflict.

Third, do not assume that you yourself are at any advanced developmental stage. (Research on ego development shows that, when people are tested and also asked what stage they think they have attained, the result is as you might guess: People consistently claim to have developed to more advanced levels than testing them indicates.)

Fourth, do not equate development with holiness. As explained several times in the text, holiness is a matter of responding wholeheartedly to the opportunities given in each present moment, and is available to the youngest as well as to the mature. Weakness, self-interest, and sin are possibilities that no amount of development will automatically cure. It may even be that the greater freedom that comes with development makes any sin more grievous.

Fifth, do not then assume that development does not matter. As also explained in chapter nine, development does offer the possibility of consistently responding more accurately and effectively to daily challenges.

Sixth, do not try to force others, or yourself, to grow. Greenhouse plants are rarely robust; forced "growth" is likely to be brittle and a self-deception.

How to Avoid Doing Harm

- *Do not claim to know more than you do about others.*
- *Do not use the language of stages and levels and transformation with anyone with whom you are in conflict.*

- *Do not assume that you yourself are at any advanced developmental stage.*
- *Do not equate development with holiness.*
- *Do not assume that development does not matter.*
- *Do not try to force others, or yourself, to grow.*

Using This Information for Your Own Well-Being

There are things that you can do for yourself with this knowledge. Here are a few:

First, appreciate the wonder of your life so far. As an infant, you lived in a world you cannot now recapture except through study; yet you developed through several of the stages described here simply by seeking to live well. Your natural curiosity as a child, your relationships with family and friends and community, and your growing responsibilities have brought you quite a long way.

Second, if you want to grow, look for opportunities. As chapter nine on spiritual practice described, there are things we can do if we wish to learn how our present mental world is incomplete. Regular reflection on our errors, difficulties, and conflicts can show us where we do not yet see accurately or know how to respond wisely. Self-discipline, especially when it involves stepping back from our impulses and easy assumptions, can help in becoming more objective and thus in emergence from our embeddedness.

Third, recognize that your environment matters. Developmental transformations seem to be spurred especially by one's exposure to people about one level beyond one's present stage. If you want to grow, you might have to examine the influence of those around you. Today especially the media you surround yourself with should be viewed with a critical eye for their (probably negative) effects. If you find yourself rarely challenged and surprised, you probably are not being helped to grow. In contrast, art and ritual can be of more help than the banalities so frequently offered by mass media. Saint Paul perhaps said it best: "Finally, beloved, whatever is true, whatever is honorable, whatever is just, whatever is pure, whatever is pleasing, whatever is commendable, if there is any excellence and if there is anything worthy of praise, think about these things" (Philippians 4:8). Great art, literature, music—these are often symbolic expressions of a mature and integrated perspective. If we put ourselves into their presence, they subtly work on us and remind us that our own present seeing is partial.

Fourth, look for guidance. This does not necessarily mean therapy, although that may be invaluable when the ordinary business of living goes awry and we find ourselves in a dead end in trying to make things better. Nor does it mean spiritual guidance, which has an aim of its own (which is not development as this book describes it). The guidance that helps us to develop is more likely to be found in informal settings. If we find people at work, in the neighborhood, or in our families who seem to be worth imitating because they have a consistently balanced, accurate, peaceful, and challenging way of meeting life each day—these are the sorts of people it may be worthwhile to cultivate as mentors or friends, or to join with in a common effort to improve our communities. If we ask sincerely, others who know and love us will often be able to point out our blind spots. As the Zen proverb says, "The Way is like a great highroad; there is no difficulty whatever in recognizing it....Just go home and plenty of people will point it out to you."[1]

Fifth, gently suspect that it is your misperception, the limits of your present developmental stage, that leads you into some of your difficulties. The ancient virtue of humility is underrated.

For Your Own Well-Being

- *Appreciate the wonder of your life so far.*
- *Reflect on your errors as possibly revealing mistaken perspectives.*
- *Examine the influence of those around you.*
- *Look for guidance.*
- *Suspect that the limits of your present developmental stage lead you into some of your difficulties.*

Using This Information Well for the Sake of Others

Our awareness of adult development can also help us in our dealings with others in our families, churches, workplaces, schools, and neighborhoods. The suggestions that follow here are to be taken lightly; even a good tool does damage when used in the wrong way.

First, appreciate that most people are doing what makes sense to them given the way they see things. There certainly are evil and selfishness in the world; but there is also a great deal of conflict and friction because we live, inevitably, in the different mental universes this book describes. Grant others as much good will as you grant yourself, for each of us acts from partial knowledge in ways we do not understand because of our embeddedness. Try to understand things from the other person's perspective, realizing that he may see the world differently from the way you do.

Second, especially with young people, recognize the limitations of their developmental level. Encourage growth rather than shaming and condemning. (This is especially important in moral and psychosexual development, since parental anxieties are often heightened in these areas.) Provide the resources that encourage development, as described above; but recognize that performance on a higher level cannot be forced.

Third, use developmental thinking when you step back from a conflict to try to understand it. Is it possible (as with the example of Ernie and his father) that a conflict cannot be resolved but only managed because those involved are living in different mental worlds? If resolution would require transformation on the part of one or another party, that outcome is unlikely. Better not to rely on it, but to seek civil accommodation without expecting the people or groups to understand each other.

Fourth, when fashioning communications that have to reach a wide audience think of the levels of development that are probably represented. As with the example of stewardship in the last chapter, people's understanding and motives vary according to the way they perceive the world—their stage of development. Recognize that what makes sense to you may not make sense to others who are at different levels, and seek to provide at least some opportunity for people at different stages to find something attractive and engaging in what you have to say.

Finally, live in hope. The promise "We will be like him" will be fulfilled in God's time and in God's way, for us and for countless others. Every step into a new developmental level is into a surprising new world, one unimaginable from our previous stage. Each stage in our development brings us more closely into tune with God's world. And God promises to meet us at our destination.

Helping Others

- *Appreciate that most people are doing what makes sense to them given the way they see things.*
- *Encourage growth rather than shaming and condemning.*
- *Use developmental thinking when you step back from a conflict to try to understand it.*
- *To reach a wide audience think of the levels of development that are probably represented.*
- *Live in hope that "we will be like him."*

Questions for Reflection and Discussion

1. Recall a conflict from your past: how might what you now know change your understanding of what happened? What might you have done differently, had you known at the time what you now know?
2. Have you set yourself tasks or goals that are now beyond you, until your development has continued further on? What might you do so as to live in peace with your present incompleteness, but not settle for it?
3. How would you describe to someone else the promise of Saint John that has been the motto throughout this book?

Notes

Introduction

1. Carl Jung, *Psychological Types*, trans. H. G. Baynes, revised by R. F. C. Hull (Princeton, NJ: Princeton University Press, 1971; original edition 1921).

2. Confucius, *To Hio: The Great Learning*, trans. Ezra Pound (Seattle: University of Washington Book Store, 1928). Quoted in Aelred Graham, *The End of Religion* (New York & London: Harcourt Brace Jovanovich, 1971), 238.

Chapter One. A Journey into Self-Knowledge

1. Rosemary Haughton, *The Passionate God* (London: Darton, Longman & Todd, 1981; and New York/Ramsey, NJ: Paulist Press, 1981), 58–59. Citations are to the Paulist edition.

2. Thomas Aquinas, *Summa Theologiae*, I, q.75, a.5.

3. Robert Kegan, *The Evolving Self* (Cambridge, MA: Harvard University Press, 1982), 31.

Chapter Two. How
Understanding Develops

1. Jean Piaget's writings are voluminous and technical. Primary sources include *The Origins of Intelligence in Children* (New York: International Universities Press, 1952; original edition 1936); and *The Construction of Reality in the Child* (New York: Basic Books, 1954; original edition 1937); and *The Moral Judgment of the Child* (Glencoe, IL: Free Press, 1948).

2. Summarized from Kegan, *Evolving Self*, 26–41.

Chapter Three. Moral Reasoning:
The Early Stages

1. Some of Lawrence Kohlberg's most salient writings can be found in his *Collected Papers on Moral Development and Moral Education* (Cambridge, MA: Center for Moral Education, 1976), and *Essays in Moral Development*, vol. 2, *The Psychology of Moral Development: Moral Stages, Their Nature and Validity* (San Francisco: Harper & Row, 1984).

2. Carol Gilligan, *In a Different Voice* (Cambridge, MA: Harvard University Press, 1983).

3. Table based on Kegan, *Evolving Self*, 34.

Chapter Five. Growing in Faith

1. The table is based on material in James Fowler's *Stages of Faith* (San Francisco: Harper & Row, 1981).

2. Fowler develops this point in *Faithful Change: The Personal and Public Challenges of Postmodern Life* (Nashville: Abingdon, 1996), chapter 10.

Chapter Six. Psychosexual Development

1. Michael Cavanagh, "The Impact of Psychosexual Growth on Marriage and Religious Life," *Human Development* 4, no. 3 (1983): 16–24.

2. Table based on Cavanagh, "Impact of Psychosexual Growth," 18.

3. Ibid., 20.

4. Ibid., 21.

Chapter Seven. Ego Development

1. Jane Loevinger, *Ego Development* (San Francisco: Jossey-Bass, 1976).

2. Table based on Loevinger, *Ego Development*, 24–25.

3. Ibid., 15–16.

4. Ibid., 19.

5. Ibid., 20–22.

6. Robert Kegan, *In Over Our Heads* (Cambridge, MA: Harvard University Press, 1994), 34.

7. Loevinger, *Ego Development*, 22–26.

8. Ibid., 26.

9. Cavanagh, "Impact of Psychosexual Growth," 21.

10. Loevinger, *Ego Development*, 26.

Chapter Eight. Taking Stock

1. Kohlberg's term, used by Kegan, *Evolving Self*, 52.

2. Loevinger, *Ego Development*, 19.

3. Fowler, *Stages of Faith*, 151.

4. See, for instance, Ken Wilber, "Structure, Stage, and Self," in *The Collected Works of Ken Wilber* (Boston & London: Shambala, 1999), 408–17.

5. James Fowler, *Faith Development and Pastoral Care* (Philadelphia: Fortress, 1987), 61–66.

6. Loevinger, *Ego Development*, 19; Fowler, *Stages of Faith*, 182; Kegan, *In Over Our Heads*, 316–55.

7. Kegan, *In Over Our Heads*, 350–52; Haughton, *Passionate God*, 60–65.

Chapter Nine. Spiritual Practice

1. Piaget, *Construction*, 41–42.

2. Gary Klein, *Sources of Power: How People Make Decisions* (Cambridge, MA & London: MIT Press, 1999), 39–40.

3. Haughton, *Passionate God*, 59.

4. Ibid., 2.

5. Richard of Chichester, "Prayer," *Catholic Forum*, http://www.catholic-forum.com/saints/saintr08.htm.

Chapter Ten. Developmental Thinking: A Practical Application

1. *Stewardship: A Disciple's Response* (Washington, DC: National Conference of Catholic Bishops / United States Catholic Conference, 1993).

2. Dean R. Hoge, Charles Zech, Patrick McNamara, and Michael J. Donahue, *Money Matters: Personal Giving in American Churches* (Louisville: Westminster John Knox, 1996); John and Sylvia Ronsvalle, *Behind the Stained Glass*

Windows: Money Dynamics in the Church (Grand Rapids: Baker Books, 1996); Robert Wuthnow, *God and Mammon in America* (New York: Free Press / Macmillan, 1994).

3. Matthew Fox, *Breakthrough: Meister Eckhart's Creation Spirituality in New Translation* (Garden City, NY: Doubleday / Image, 1980), 202.

Chapter Eleven. Putting What We Know to Work

1. R. H. Blyth, *Zen in English Literature and Oriental Classics* (Tokyo: Hokuseido Press, 1942), 20–21. Quoted in Aelred Graham, *Zen Catholicism: A Suggestion* (New York: Harcourt, Brace, & World, 1963), 50.

For Further Reading

The Process of Transformation

This book takes its cue about transformation from the work of Rosemary Haughton in *The Transformation of Man* (London: Geoffrey Chapman; and Springfield, IL: Templegate, 1967) and *The Passionate God* (London: Darton, Longman & Todd; and New York and Ramsey, NJ: Paulist Press, 1981). The most profound work on transformation (called "conversion" by him) is by the Canadian philosopher Bernard Lonergan, but his classic *Insight* (New York: Philosophical Library, 1957) is as exceedingly difficult as it is rewarding. A good introduction to Lonergan can be found in Tad Dunne's *Lonergan and Spirituality* (Chicago: Loyola University Press, 1985) which is much more accessible, although still not easy to read. The psychiatrist George Valliant has written two books on development through the lifespan that are descriptively fascinating, although more from a mental health and psychoanalytic perspective than the developmental one outlined here: *Adaptation to Life* (Boston: Little, Brown, 1977), and *The Wisdom of the Ego* (Cambridge, MA: Harvard University Press, 1993).

Early Developmental Thinking

Modern psychological thought about adult development began with the Swiss psychiatrist Carl Jung, but because of the sprawling nature of his work he is best approached through his interpreters. The best single-volume summary is Edward Whitmont's *The Symbolic Quest* (New York: G. P. Putnam's Sons / C. G. Jung Foundation, 1969). Readers interested in the relationship of Jung to Catholic faith can consult *Catholicism and Jungian Psychology*, edited by J. Marvin Spiegelman (Tempe, AZ: New Falcon, 1994). Erik Erikson's major works are *Childhood and Society* (New York: W. W. Norton & Company, revised and enlarged edition 1963), and *Identity: Youth and Crisis* (New York: W. W. Norton & Company, 1968).

Daniel Levinson's findings on development through the lifespan are contained in *The Seasons of a Man's Life* (New York: Alfred A. Knopf, 1968), popularized by Gail Sheehy in *Passages* (New York: E. P. Dutton, 1976); and, in collaboration with Judy D. Levinson, *The Seasons of a Woman's Life* (New York: Alfred A. Knopf, 1996).

Cognitive and Moral Development

Much of the work by Piaget and Kohlberg is too technical even to be a second step after this book. But Robert Kegan's *The Evolving Self* (Cambridge, MA: Harvard University Press, 1982) provides excellent material on both, plus an extensive reference list for those who would like to go more deeply into original sources. The critique of Kohlberg's work which questions the applicability of the content of his theory to women can be found in Carol Gilligan's *In a Different Voice* (Cambridge, MA: Harvard

University Press, 1983). A philosopher's perspective on the growth of moral responsibility that may interest readers is Herbert Fingarette's *Mapping Responsibility* (Chicago and LaSalle, IL: Open Court, 2004), especially chapter 1.

Faith Development

The primary source remains James Fowler's *Stages of Faith* (San Francisco: Harper & Row, 1981). He offers a more technical analysis and application to practical theology in *Faith Development and Pastoral Care* (Philadelphia: Fortress, 1987). His *Becoming Adult, Becoming Christian* (San Francisco: Jossey-Bass, 2000) puts the developmental material into a context of vocation and explicit Christian faith. And readers with an interest in the application of faith development theory to contemporary society and the "culture wars" can find Fowler's comments on this topic in Part III of his *Faithful Change: The Personal and Public Challenges of Postmodern Life* (Nashville: Abingdon, 1996). His current reflections on the implications of his theory are laid out in "Faith Development at 30: Naming the Challenges of Faith in a New Millennium," *Religious Education* 99, no. 4 (Fall, 2004): 405–21.

One rare example of the application of structural-developmental thinking to religious living can be found in Elizabeth Liebert's *Changing Life Patterns: Adult Development in Spiritual Direction* (New York/Mahwah, NJ: Paulist, 1992). The topic of faith development is approached from a perspective based more on the work of Erik Erikson in two books by Evelyn Eaton Whitehead and James Whitehead, *Christian Life Patterns* (New edition: New York: Crossroad, 1992) and their more elementary *Christian Adulthood* (Ligouri, MO: Ligouri, 2005). An application of Fowler's work to the development of faith specifically during the college and young-adult years can be found in Sharon Parks's *The Critical Years: The Young Adult Search for a Faith to Live By* (New York: Harper & Row, 1986).

Psychosexual Development

Michael Cavanagh's original article "The Impact of Psychosexual Growth on Marriage and Religious Life," *Human Development* 4, no. 3 (1983): 16–24, is the source of the stage and phase outline. An excellent amplification of this work can be found in *Your Sexual Self* by Fran Ferder and John Heagle (Notre Dame, IN: Ave Maria, 1992). These authors have another volume on the spirituality of sexuality, *Tender Fires: The Spiritual Promise of Sexuality* (New York: Crossroad, 2002). A book that could be read as treating psychosexual development autobiographically is Lauren F. Winner's memoir-like *Real Sex: The Naked Truth about Chastity* (Grand Rapids: Brazos, 2005).

Ego Development

Interested (and determined) readers with some background in psychology might find the first several chapters of Jane Loevinger's classic *Ego Development* (San Francisco: Jossey-Bass, 1976) worth the effort. Robert Kegan's book *In Over Our Heads* (Cambridge, MA: Harvard University Press, 1994) vividly demonstrates how the increasing complexity of contemporary society requires increasingly complex development. Two fascinating contemporary books on development, although ranging more widely than the material here, are by Judith Rich Harris, *The Nurture Assumption: Why Children Turn Out the Way They Do* (New York: Simon & Schuster/

Touchstone, 1998), and *No Two Alike: Human Nature and Human Individuality* (New York: W. W. Norton, 2006). This latter book also opens the door to exploring the neurological basis for development.

Stewardship and Development

The pastoral letter *Stewardship: A Disciple's Response* is published by the United States Conference of Catholic Bishops (Washington, DC: NCCB/USCC, 1993). A spiritual perspective on money that comes from a very different religious tradition but that has some intriguing parallels with the approach to development outlined here can be found summarized in Karl H. Potter's article "Four Indian Attitudes toward Money," *Parabola* 16, no. 1 (1991): 87–92. An empirical and theological analysis of motives for giving (although not within the developmental framework of this book) can be found in *Money Matters: Personal Giving in American Churches* by Dean R. Hoge, Charles Zech, Patrick McNamara, and Michael J. Donahue (Louisville: Westminster John Knox, 1996), especially chapter 6. Further research and analysis of religious affiliation and economic behavior are described in Robert Wuthnow's *God and Mammon in America* (New York: Free Press / Macmillan, 1994) and, with special attention to power relationships expressed through money, in John and Sylvia Ronsvalle's *Behind the Stained Glass Windows: Money Dynamics in the Church* (Grand Rapids: Baker Books, 1996).

Other Topics

Those who found the examples of language development intriguing would vastly enjoy Steven Pinker's *Words and Rules: The Ingredients of Language* (New York: Basic Books, 1999). The example in chapter 9 about neonatal intensive care nurses is taken from a fascinating book on how experts make decisions, *Sources of Power* by Gary Klein (Cambridge, MA: MIT Press, 1998), 39–40. And for those with a historical interest specifically in constructivist psychology, the first volume of George Kelly's *The Psychology of Personal Constructs* (Two volumes: New York: W. W. Norton, 1955) is a technical, yet surprisingly easy to read and provocative, introduction.